Your Right to Child Custody, Visitation, and Support

Fourth Edition

Mary L. Boland

Attorney at Law

SPHINX® PUBLISHING
AN IMPRINT OF SOURCEBOOKS, INC.®
NAPERVILLE, ILLINOIS
www.SphinxLegal.com

Fourth Edition: 2007

Published by: Sphinx® Publishing, An Imprint of Sourcebooks, Inc.®

Naperville Office
P.O. Box 4410
Naperville, Illinois 60567-4410
630-961-3900
Fax: 630-961-2168
www.sourcebooks.com
www.SphinxLegal.com

This publication is designed to provide accurate and authoritative information in regard to the subject matter covered. It is sold with the understanding that the publisher is not engaged in rendering legal, accounting, or other professional service. If legal advice or other expert assistance is required, the services of a competent professional person should be sought.

From a Declaration of Principles Jointly Adopted by a Committee of the American Bar Association and a Committee of Publishers and Associations

This product is not a substitute for legal advice.

Disclaimer required by Texas statutes.

Library of Congress Cataloging-in-Publication Data
Boland, Mary L.
  Your right to child custody, visitation, and support / by Mary L. Boland.
-- 4th ed.
      p. cm.
  Includes index.
  ISBN-13: 978-1-57248-582-2 (pbk. : alk. paper)
  ISBN-10: 1-57248-582-5 (pbk. : alk. paper)
  1. Custody of children--United States--Popular works. 2. Visitation rights (Domestic relations)--United States--Popular works. 3. Child support--Law and legislation--United States--Popular works. I. Title.

KF547.Z9B65 2007
346.7301'73--dc22
                                                        2006035061

Printed and bound in the United States of America.
SB — 10 9 8 7 6 5 4 3 2 1

Contents

Using Self-Help Law Books vii

Introduction xi

Chapter 1: Preliminary Considerations 1
   The Role of the Law
   Legal Research
   The Role of Lawyers
   Firing Your Lawyer

**Chapter 2: Understanding Custody
        and Visitation** 13
   Custody and Visitation—Generally
   Getting Custody
   Taxes and Custody

**Chapter 3: The Law of Custody and Visitation:
        Best Interests of the Child** 19
   Best Interests Between Parents
   Factors Considered
   Factors in Deciding Visitation

Nonparents and Custody
Nonparents and Visitation

Chapter 4: Developing Your Parenting Plan........35
Formulating an Agreement
Joint Custody
Joint Parenting Agreements
Custody and Visitation Checklist of Factors to Consider

Chapter 5: Filing Your Case 47
Preparation for Your Case
Parental Information
Information about Your Child
Gathering and Saving the Documents
Who Can File
What You Must Prove
Where to File
What to File
Filing Fees and Other Costs
The Petition for Custody or Visitation
The Summons and Service
Responding to a Petition for Custody or Visitation
Temporary Custody or Visitation
The Next Step

Chapter 6: Resolving Your Case Without a Trial: Mediation 63
Working on an Agreement
Mediation
Finding a Mediation Program
Preparing for Mediation
The Mediator
Settling the Case
When Mediation May Not Be Appropriate
When the Parties Do Not Agree

Chapter 7: The Contested Custody Case 77
Background
Discovery

Court Procedures
Final Judgment

Chapter 8: Kidnapping, Abuse, Visitation Problems, and Other Emergencies............... 89

Kidnapping
Domestic Violence and Child Abuse
Visitation Problems

Chapter 9: Child Support 97

History of Child Support
The Basics
How Support is Determined
Factors in Setting Child Support

Chapter 10: Child Support Agreements.......... 117

Factors to Consider
The Appropriate Guideline
Your Basic Guideline Amount
Your Child Support Amount
Writing Your Agreement
Duration of the Order
Payments
Health Care
Life Insurance
Tax Exemption
Sample Combined Income Child Support Worksheet
Sample Percentage of Income Child Support Worksheet

Chapter 11: The Child Support Case 131

Gathering Financial Information
Filing for Child Support
Finding and Notifying a Parent
Establishing Parentage (if Necessary)
Following Court Procedures
Responding to a Petition for Child Support

Chapter 12: Modification, Termination,
and Appeal **141**
Modification
Termination
Appeal
The Future

Glossary **153**

Appendix A: Sample, Filled-In Forms **159**

Appendix B: Blank Forms **195**

Index **269**

Using Self-Help Law Books

Before using a self-help law book, you should realize the advantages and disadvantages of doing your own legal work and understand the challenges and diligence that this requires.

The Growing Trend

Rest assured that you will not be the first or only person handling your own legal matter. For example, in some states, more than 75% of the people in divorces and other cases represent themselves. Because of the high cost of legal services, this is a major trend, and many courts are struggling to make it easier for people to represent themselves. However, some courts are not happy with people who do not use attorneys and refuse to help them in any way. For some, the attitude is, "Go to the law library and figure it out for yourself."

We write and publish self-help law books to give people an alternative to the often complicated and confusing legal books found in most law libraries. We have made the explanations of the law as simple and easy to understand as possible. Of course, unlike an attorney advising an individual client, we cannot cover every conceivable possibility.

Cost/Value Analysis

Whenever you shop for a product or service, you are faced with various levels of quality and price. In deciding what product or service to buy, you make a cost/value analysis on the basis of your willingness to pay and the quality you desire.

When buying a car, you decide whether you want transportation, comfort, status, or sex appeal. Accordingly, you decide among choices such as a Neon, a Lincoln, a Rolls Royce, or a Porsche. Before making a decision, you usually weigh the merits of each option against the cost.

When you get a headache, you can take a pain reliever (such as aspirin) or visit a medical specialist for a neurological examination. Given this choice, most people, of course, take a pain reliever, since it costs only pennies; whereas a medical examination costs hundreds of dollars and takes a lot of time. This is usually a logical choice because it is rare to need anything more than a pain reliever for a headache. But in some cases, a headache may indicate a brain tumor, and failing to see a specialist right away can result in complications. Should everyone with a headache go to a specialist? Of course not, but people treating their own illnesses must realize that they are betting, on the basis of their cost/value analysis of the situation, that they are taking the most logical option.

The same cost/value analysis must be made when deciding to do one's own legal work. Many legal situations are very straightforward, requiring a simple form and no complicated analysis. Anyone with a little intelligence and a book of instructions can handle the matter without outside help.

But there is always the chance that complications are involved that only an attorney would notice. To simplify the law into a book like this, several legal cases often must be condensed into a single sentence or paragraph. Otherwise, the book would be several hundred pages long and too complicated for most people. However, this simplification necessarily leaves out many details and nuances that would apply to special or unusual situations. Also, there are many ways to interpret most legal questions. Your case may come before a judge who disagrees with the analysis of our authors.

Therefore, in deciding to use a self-help law book and to do your own legal work, you must realize that you are making a cost/value analysis. You have decided that the money you will save in doing it yourself outweighs the chance that your case will not turn out to your satisfaction. Most people handling their own simple legal matters never have a problem, but occasionally people find that it ended up costing them more to have an attorney straighten out the situation than it would have if they had hired an attorney in the beginning. Keep this in mind while handling your case, and be sure to consult an attorney if you feel you might need further guidance.

Local Rules   The next thing to remember is that a book which covers the law for the entire nation, or even for an entire state, cannot possibly include every procedural difference of every jurisdiction. Whenever possible, we provide the exact form needed; however, in some areas, each county, or even each judge, may require unique forms and procedures. In our state books, our forms usually cover the majority of counties in the state or provide examples of the type of form that will be required. In our national books, our forms are sometimes even more general in nature but are designed to give a good idea of the type of form that will be needed in most locations. Nonetheless, keep in mind that your state, county, or judge may have a requirement, or use a form, that is not included in this book.

You should not necessarily expect to be able to get all of the information and resources you need solely from within the pages of this book. This book will serve as your guide, giving you specific information whenever possible and helping you to find out what else you will need to know. This is just like if you decided to build your own backyard deck. You might purchase a book on how to build decks. However, such a book would not include the building codes and permit requirements of every city, town, county, and township in the nation; nor would it include the lumber, nails, saws, hammers, and other materials and tools you would need to actually build the deck. You would use the book as your guide, and then do some work and research involving such matters as whether you need a permit of some kind, what type and grade of wood is available in your area, whether to use hand tools or power tools, and how to use those tools.

Before using the forms in a book like this, you should check with your court clerk to see if there are any local rules of which you should be aware or local forms you will need to use. Often, such forms will require the same information as the forms in the book but are merely laid out differently or use slightly different language. They will sometimes require additional information.

Changes in the Law

Besides being subject to local rules and practices, the law is subject to change at any time. The courts and the legislatures of all fifty states are constantly revising the laws. It is possible that while you are reading this book, some aspect of the law is being changed.

In most cases, the change will be of minimal significance. A form will be redesigned, additional information will be required, or a waiting period will be extended. As a result, you might need to revise a form, file an extra form, or wait out a longer time period. These types of changes will not usually affect the outcome of your case. On the other hand, sometimes a major part of the law is changed, the entire law in a particular area is rewritten, or a case that was the basis of a central legal point is overruled. In such instances, your entire ability to pursue your case may be impaired.

Introduction

The issues of custody and visitation arise most often in divorce proceedings and can be the biggest contest between parents. More than 40% of marriages end in divorce, affecting about one million children every year.

Children often feel caught in the middle of these contests. One program in New Jersey, called *Kids Count*, has offered parents an opportunity to see how much pain a contested custody battle imposes on kids. As reported in an article about one court-run program, children were invited to draw pictures and write letters. One child drew a tug-of-war with the child as the object; some drew faces with enormous tears. One wrote a letter to her mother in which she told her that she hated her mother "when you drink too much and can't take care of me." Many asked their parents to get back together, or expressed their fear and said they were sorry they were bad. When kids were asked to complete the question, "what if...," their responses included: What if I find out my parents have been lying to me about almost everything? What if my dad takes me out after he hit my head against a wall? What if my dad takes my mom again and chokes her again? What if my birthday comes and both my parents forget? What if I come home from school and no one is home?[*]

[*]*See* Bari Zell-Weinberger, "A New Program in New Jersey Helps Attorneys Protect Children's Interests in Divorce Disputes." *Matrimonial Strategist*. June 10, 2003, vol.21, no.5, pg.3.

Custody may also be an issue when the parents have never married. Roughly one million children are born to unwed mothers each year. Marriage or not, child support can be more than a hotly contested issue—it can also lead to long-term enforcement problems. Knowledge of the legal process and an understanding of the laws in this area can help reduce the acrimony involved in these cases, and ultimately increase the willingness of both parents to be actively committed to their children emotionally, physically, and financially.

Because of the importance of the decision and the possible need for expert witnesses, child custody battles are often a very expensive part of a divorce. The goal of this book is to help you consider your options in deciding custody, visitation, and child support questions by giving you a broad overview of the factors that courts examine when determining these issues. While every family has the same basic needs, every family is also unique. Perhaps the overriding concept in this area of law is that decisions, whether based on an agreement of the parents or determined after trial, should be made with the maximum flexibility to accommodate a particular family's needs within certain minimum guidelines.

Thus, as you read the chapters that follow, do not seek out a *boiler-plate* answer to fit every situation. Rather, this book provides you with the necessary ingredients to be successful in working towards your goals, whether they be for full custody, a joint arrangement, flexible visitation, or appropriate child support.

Additionally, keep in mind that there are no absolute *winners* in these cases. Your objective is to be heard and to have your concerns considered fairly, especially in a contested case where each parent would be seen by a court as a potentially appropriate caretaker and supporter of a child. The most important consideration of any decision in this area is that it be in the best interests of your child.

Chapters 1–4 of this book explain the procedures for obtaining custody of your child. Included is an explanation of the *best interests standards* and different options for determining custody. Information for filing your custody case can be found in Chapter 5. Chapter 6 provides a detailed explanation of the mediation process, while Chapter 7 covers what to do if mediation doesn't work and you end up in a contested custody case. Chapters 9–11 take you through the filing for child support. An explanation of child support guideline factors used in determining support can be found in Chapter 10, and procedures for filing your case are found in Chapter 11. Modification of custody and child support is covered in Chapter 12.

Appendix A gives you an example of what a fictional case looks like through the forms used. Finally, Appendix B includes blank forms you can use as models or modify as needed.

For additional information, you can use the Internet and go online to **www.sphinxlegal.com/extras/rightstochildcustody**, where you can find specific information on the laws of your state concerning child custody and support, as well as links to each states' child support enforcement agency.

Preliminary Considerations

Custody and visitation laws have undergone considerable changes in the last twenty years in the United States. While child custody laws developed for resolving parenting issues between divorcing husbands and wives, today, these laws are being reshaped and applied to traditional and nontraditional family units where the custody or visitation of a child must be determined. With the high rates of divorce, many families are blended together, with each spouse bringing children to the new marriage. Couples may have a child in common, but have never married and have never lived together. Grandparents or extended family members become the custodians of children. Same-sex parents also have children.

The birth of a child brings long-term responsibilities to the parents. All parents, married or not, have a duty to provide reasonable care, financial support, and disciplinary guidelines for their child. Even so, not all parents share the same views on child rearing and not all parents define the word *responsible* the same way. It is also true that parents often disagree on how much financial support is necessary, especially when it is the subject of a court order.

If the parents have been married, these differences are heightened during divorce proceedings, when custody, visitation, and child support all become issues to be resolved. If the parents have never been married, these differences may be even greater, since the parents may have never even considered or shared their views on children with one another. The father may not even be certain that he is, in fact, the father. Also, an unmarried parent may feel little responsibility for a child not in his or her daily care. This is most often the case with a father, especially if his relationship with the child's mother ends during, or shortly after, the onset of her pregnancy.

THE ROLE OF THE LAW

Once a child custody, visitation, or support matter is brought to the courts, there is a continuing duty under the law for the court to watch over the child, almost like a *super parent*. The good news is, though, that parents who agree on the terms of care and support for their child will usually see a court adopt their agreement. Ultimately, the law in your jurisdiction will govern what kinds of agreements you can make and what kinds of orders are entered.

When parents contest these matters, courts have developed various strategies to address the difficult task of considering a unique relationship and weighing what is in the best interests of the child. However, there are nearly as many variations within the legal guidelines in custody, visitation, and support provisions as there are families.

The legal factors and guidelines are intentionally broad and generalized because the parent-child relationship is not so easily captured on paper with set times, places, and amounts. Yet, to some extent, that is what the law of child custody, visitation, and support is about—the effort to reduce the intangible relationships between parent and child to some definable level of interaction and support. This is why it is important, whenever possible, to try to work out an agreement that recognizes that both of you want the best for your child and that provides the maximum flexibility under the law to allow you to succeed in being good parents. A great number of contested custody cases can be resolved with an agreement when the parents are willing to discuss the options.

LEGAL RESEARCH

Every state has passed a set of *statutes* or *codes* that co
laws passed by the legislature. A portion of the statutes or
set forth the standards for determining custody, visitation, and child
support. To find the laws for your state and to properly prepare the
necessary paperwork, you will need to do some basic legal research.

Law Libraries

A large public library may carry some legal books, but a specialized
law library will have the most up-to-date versions of your state's laws,
as well as other types of research materials not found in a regular
public library. Law libraries can usually be found at or near your local
courthouse. Your court clerk's office should be able to tell you where to
find the law library. Also, any law school will have a law library.

Contact the closest law library to determine hours and directions.
Also, ask if there are any restrictions on use of the library by
members of the general public. Some law libraries may have limitations (such as limited hours or days) for non-attorneys, and law school
libraries may have similar (or stricter) restrictions for nonstudents.

Statutes or Codes

Your first step will probably be to find the basic law in your
state's statutes or codes. The actual title of the set of books
containing the statutes or codes is very important. For example,
Arizona Revised Statutes Annotated or *Delaware Code Annotated*.
Once you find the proper set of books, look for the section, title, or
other numbers listed for your state in order to find the exact provisions of the law. Reference librarians are very good and can help you
find the correct set of books.

For example, if you look at the listing for Illinois, you will see the
following notation after the heading The Law: *West's Illinois
Compiled Statutes Annotated, Chapter 750, Article 5, Section 602 (750
ILCS 5/602).* This gives you the title of the set of books (*West's Illinois
Compiled Statutes Annotated*). You will also note the following notation under the heading *Custody: 750 ILCS 5/602.* This tells you that
the the portion of the Illinois law relating to custody is found in
Chapter 750 of the set of books called the *Illinois Compiled Statutes,*
and begins with Article 5, Section 602. The legal *citation* (abbreviation)
for this would be *750 ILCS 5/602*, where "750" refers to Chapter 750,
"ILCS" is the abbreviation for Illinois Compiled Statutes, and "5/602"
refers to Article 5, Section 602.

Once you locate the specific laws for your state, check to see if there is a more current version available. This may be in the form of an update inserted in the back of the volume, a separate update volume, or in some other format. If necessary, ask a reference librarian for assistance in order to be certain you have the most recent version. The statutes may also be *annotated* with short summaries of court decisions that have interpreted the statutes.

At **www.sphinxlegal.com/extras/rightstochildcustody**, you can find information on the titles of the set of books for your state.

Case Reporters

If you wish to find the court's entire decision, it will be included in a state or regional *case reporter*. A state case reporter, such as the *Illinois Reporter*, contains court opinions from the courts of a single state. A regional reporter, such as the *Northeastern Reporter*, contains cases from the courts of several states in a certain geographic area. To find a case, carefully copy down the case name and the numbers that follow it (called the *citation*) or make a copy of the page containing the case information. Next, locate the case reporters in the library. Many states have more than one reporter in which the same case can be found. Again, ask a librarian for assistance. The citation often looks as follows.

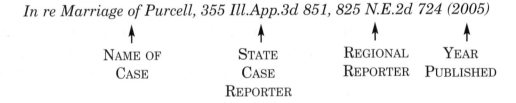

Once you find the proper state or regional reporter, the case is found using the following method.

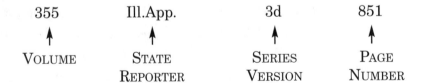

You will find the Illinois appellate court opinion in the case of *In re marriage of Purcell* in volume 355 of the state reporter titled *Illinois Appellate Reporter, Third Series*, on page 857.

After a point, instead of continuing to increase the volume publishers have started over with volume one of a subsequ of the reporter. In our example, you would actually find th books on the library shelves: one titled *Illinois Appellate Reporter*, another titled *Illinois Appellate Reporter, Second Series*; and a third titled *Illinois Appellate Reporter, Third Series*. Each set begins with Volume 1. The *Third Series* contains the most recent cases.

Internet Research

Increasingly, the Internet is becoming a resource to obtain legal information specific to the various states. Many states include their statutes (and selected cases) on their government Web pages. One easy way to find available Web information on the laws of your state is to begin by searching the LawCrawler search engine by Findlaw. Type in **www.findlaw.com**, then choose state cases and codes to search your state. The listing of the Office of Child Support Enforcement state websites can be found at **www.acf.dhhs.gov/ programs/cse**. It provides links to states that have their own child support home pages. Some states also include family law forms on the Internet.

Researching on the Internet can be much faster than looking up your state's laws in the books, but online research produces only a screen snapshot at a time, so you may need to open several pages to see the whole picture of your state's custody, visitation, or support laws. Also, be aware that information on a website may not be the most current version of the law. When working online, be sure to review all of the relevant website information, then download or print the portion of the law in which you are interested.

Legal Encyclopedia

You should also be able to find sets of books called *legal encyclopedias* at a law library. These are similar to regular encyclopedias, in that you look up the subject (such as "Custody" or "Divorce"), and it gives you a summary of the law on that subject, along with citations to court cases that relate to that subject.

There are two national legal encyclopedias. One is *American Jurisprudence* (Am.Jur.), and the other is *Corpus Juris Secundum* (C.J.S.). Many states also have their own encyclopedia, such as *Florida Jurisprudence* (Fla.Jur.) and *Texas Jurisprudence* (Tex.Jur.). Like the case reporters, these may also have a second series.

Digests   Another type of book found in law libraries is called a *digest*. Like a legal encyclopedia, you look up the subject, but instead of giving you a summary of the law, it gives you summaries of court cases discussing that subject of the law. Although a national digest exists, it involves a very time-consuming search. You should look for a digest that is specific for your state, for example, *California Digest*. Again, there may be a second series.

Form and Practice Manuals   All law libraries also have certain form and practice manuals that include the law, procedures, and forms used in your state. These can be most helpful in both preparing your forms and finding forms you may need that are not included in this book. Never hesitate to ask a reference librarian for assistance in finding the practice section for family law in your local legal library.

THE ROLE OF LAWYERS

Cases involving child custody, visitation, and support are considered *civil* cases (as distinguished from *criminal* cases). For many years, if a party wanted a lawyer in a civil case, the party would have to get and pay for one themselves. That is still often true today.

In some cases, though, the effort to make parents responsible for child support has led to collection laws enforced by government attorneys. The issues of custody and visitation may also be decided as part of the process. Additionally, in cases where the parents have not married, the parentage of the child may first need to be established in order to proceed with the custody, visitation, and support issues. (See Appendix A and later chapters on child support for more information.)

For most parents, cases involving the issues of child custody and visitation are filed by the parties without the assistance of a government attorney. In these cases, it is still up to the parties to decide whether or not they want to be represented by a lawyer. When choosing a lawyer, recognize that the law is a business as well as a profession. This usually means that if you want a lawyer to help you obtain custody or visitation, or help you seek to establish or collect child support, you will usually have to pay for one. However, if you are without funds to pay for an attorney, a court may order the parent with the most financial resources to pay for the attorney's fees of the other parent. Be sure to discuss this issue with any lawyer you consider hiring. If the lawyer believes you may qualify, he or she will file the necessary papers to ask the judge to order the other party to pay for your lawyer.

As you are analyzing your options with a lawyer, the lawyer is likely to be evaluating your case. Lawyers decide whether to take cases based on a number of factors that include not only the costs, time, and effort, but also their potential for collection of fees.

Confidentiality

To encourage people to speak freely to their lawyers, the law provides confidentiality protection for clients. This is called the *attorney-client privilege*. This privilege prevents a lawyer from disclosing your information under most circumstances, so be honest in disclosing all the facts, even those facts about your marriage, your relationship with the other parent, or yourself that may be embarrassing or humiliating. Your lawyer may need this information to properly evaluate the case and to effectively represent you.

Finding a Lawyer

The search for a lawyer can take some time and perseverance. Just as other professions are becoming more specialized, it is becoming rarer today to find a lawyer that has a general practice. Make sure that the lawyer you choose has some kind of experience with child custody and support cases. Many lawyers limit their practice to *family law* cases, which include cases involving divorce, custody, visitation, and child support. Some states certify lawyers as *specialists*. (For example, California qualifies certain lawyers as specialists in family law.)

Recommendations from friends. Many times a lawyer is chosen on the strength of recommendations by family or friends. These recommendations can be helpful because the good experience of your family member or friend may provide reliable information on the quality of service provided by the lawyer.

Referral services. If you do not personally know a lawyer and do not have a recommendation from a trusted friend or family member, you can look to other sources. In most cities, there are organizations called *bar associations*, to which many attorneys belong. Many local or state bar associations offer a referral service.

Yellow Pages and other advertisements. You may also search for a lawyer by examining advertisements. Sometimes lawyers list their practice in the Yellow Pages of the phone book under "Lawyers" or "Attorneys." Some may advertise in newspapers or on billboards. You may even read about a lawyer's representation of another child custody, visitation, or support case in the newspaper or see something about it on television.

Prepaid legal plans. If you are a member of a prepaid legal plan, you may be covered for family law matters. Under such a plan, you may qualify for a certain number of options, such as a certain amount of hours of consultation or services, a reduced payment fee for certain services, or coverage for certain basic services like an uncontested divorce.

Websites. Another place to search for a lawyer is on the Internet. Some lawyers now have Web pages and list their services and contact information. Even if you do not have access to the Internet at home, many public libraries have Internet computers for use by library patrons.

Legal clinics. In cities with larger populations, there are often legal clinics that provide lower-cost legal representation in family law matters. Low-income persons may also qualify for free legal representation.

Law schools. Some law schools maintain clinical programs that take cases. Be sure to check with any local law schools to see if any programs exist and if your case would be eligible for the service. If the clinic does accept your case, your fee may be waived or your payment may be based on a sliding fee scale according to your income level.

Attorney registration. Every state maintains a registration of lawyers who practice law within that state. To find the phone number and address of any lawyer within your state, contact the bar association or any other attorney registration office within your state.

Initial Contact   The selection of a lawyer usually begins with a phone call to the lawyer's office. In this first contact with the lawyer, be sure to ask some preliminary information questions. Write down the information as it is given to you. Some questions to ask are—Does this lawyer charge for a consultation? How long will the first meeting be? How much does the lawyer usually charge for his or her services? Compare the answers given by all the lawyers to whom you have spoken and then decide which one to meet with for an introductory consultation.

First Interview

The first interview with a lawyer is very important. Remember that you have not agreed to anything other than the terms of the initial visit. Do not be intimidated by the thought of meeting with the lawyer. You are under no obligation to sign or agree to anything at this time, and you can take any written documents home to think about before you sign. Also, be sure to write down any information you obtain from the lawyer. It will help you remember who said what later.

Follow your instincts and trust your evaluation of the lawyer when you meet. Do you like this lawyer? Do you feel that he or she is listening to you? Does he or she appear to understand your situation? Are you treated with respect during your visit by the office staff? Your gut is the most reliable source in deciding whether you wish to proceed further with this lawyer.

In telling the lawyer about your case, be as clear and concise as possible. You will want to bring any relevant documents (see Chapters 4 and 5) that will help the lawyer to understand the facts of your case. Discuss what the lawyer thinks the projected costs will be, how you will be billed for those costs, and what payment arrangements can be made.

Fee Arrangements

In most family law cases, attorneys charge hourly fees in addition to the expenses of the case. Most attorneys are expensive, charging more than $100 per hour, and may require a substantial initial payment (sometimes called a *retainer*) from you to begin the case.

If a retainer is to be paid, make sure that you and your lawyer agree what minimum services are to be provided for that sum. For example, for a retainer of $500 or more, the lawyer should at least prepare and file your case and have the initial papers (usually a petition or complaint and a summons) served on the other parent. What you want to avoid is a situation where you pay your lawyer a retainer, he or she writes a letter and makes a few phone calls to the other parent (or the parent's attorney), then tells you the retainer is used up and more money is required from you to continue your case.

In collection of past-due child support, some states permit attorneys to charge a percentage of the judgment collected (usually one-third). If no monies are collected, no fees will be due (but you will still be responsible for the expenses of filing the documents, photocopying, telephone charges, postage, transcript, reporter, and service fees).

However your fee is arranged, make sure that you have it in writing so that there is no confusion as to what is and what is not included in the attorney's fee, what is owed, and when and how it should be paid.

Working with Your Lawyer

Once you decide to hire the lawyer and the lawyer agrees to take the case, be sure to let the lawyer know what kind of client you are. How involved do you want to be in the case? Do you want to be informed of each step in the case? Would you like copies of each document the lawyer files or receives in your case? (Realize that you may be expected to pay for photocopies.) Alternatively, you may ask your lawyer to make the file available to you on a regular basis to view at his or her office to keep current with developments in your case.

Your lawyer should be able to take you through the case step-by-step to explain the procedures and anticipated timeline. Ask the lawyer how often you can expect him or her to contact you about your case. If you know the general timeline of your case, it will help you understand how often to expect contact from the lawyer.

Once your documents are filed with the court, it may be at least thirty days before the other parent is required to file any response. Set up a method of contact that is convenient for you and reasonable for your lawyer. Many problems that arise between a client and lawyer in family law cases could easily be resolved by clear communications between the client and his or her lawyer.

FIRING YOUR LAWYER

You are entitled to reasonable communication with your lawyer, and you have a right to expect competent legal counsel. If you are not happy with your lawyer, you may choose to end his or her services at any time. Be aware, however, that the lawyer will be entitled to payment for services already provided. Also, if papers have been filed in court, the lawyer may have to get the court's permission to withdraw from the case. If the problem is communication, you might try to work it out before firing the lawyer, because getting a second lawyer will cost you another retainer and more expenses, not to mention the time spent bringing the second lawyer up to date on the case.

If you believe your lawyer has acted unethically, you may contact the state's registration agency. Each state agency regulates lawyer practices. The American Bar Association maintains a listing of all state registration agencies in its Center for Professional Responsibility. You can find the list at **www.abanet.org/cpr/regulation/home/html**.

If you are not sure whether your lawyer is acting properly, talk to another lawyer to get a second opinion. The easiest way to terminate your lawyer's services is to hire another lawyer. The new lawyer will contact the old one and get your file and the necessary paperwork completed. However, if you have not yet gotten another lawyer, and you want to fire your current one, make sure you do it in writing, and unless you hand-deliver it, send it certified or registered mail.

In the letter, you can list the problem or simply state that "as of __ date, your services are terminated." You should seek to get a copy of your file. In some states, the lawyer has a right to be paid before he or she releases the file. If you can't pay the bill in full, discuss it with your lawyer to see if you can work out a payment plan, or contact your state bar association to see if they can assist you.

Understanding Custody and Visitation

As the face of the family continues to evolve in the United States, so does the law with respect to custody and visitation. In the 1970s, about 80% of family households were made up of a married father and mother, and their own children. Census bureau figures show that today, the traditional mother-father-child family exists in only about one-third of households. The high rates of divorce rates during the 1970s and 80s led to a high percentage of blended families, as new spouses brought their children with them when they remarried. Today, blended families comprise over 30% of family households. Another ten million men and women live together without marriage, and in about half of these cases, they have a child in common. There are also another ten million families headed by single mothers, and another two million headed by single fathers. Between one and six million more children are being raised in same-sex parent households. These nontraditional families may have their own biological child, may have adopted, or may have conceived through artificial insemination.

Custody laws were originally concerned with a married mother and father, and their own children. Historically, from as far back as early Roman times, children were seen as the property of their parents. In the United States, fathers held the rights to control their children until the mid-1800s. However, as the country became more industrialized, a shift took place, and until the middle part of this century, courts usually held that a mother was the most appropriate custodian for a child, especially a young child. This was called the *tender-years doctrine*.

Today, many fathers successfully seek custody of their children because the emphasis is now on who is the best caretaker for the child. This is one reason why it is very important that the person seeking custody of a child has a history of full participation in the child's life. In many cases, the mother has been the primary caretaker for the child, so when a custody contest arises, a court may still award custody to the mother.

With the changing face of family, custody laws today have also had to address situations where the breakup of a blended families means that a stepparent, who has become the *de facto parent* to the child, seeks custody. Grandparents, too, are increasingly seeking custody or visitation with their grandchildren. Same-sex parents and surrogates (a woman who carries a baby for another) are also posing new challenges to the law. Persons who have been a significant part of raising a child may be functioning as a *psychological parent*, if not a legal parent, and they may also attempt to claim a right to the care or custody of a child.

When custody questions arise between two natural parents, the law examines what is in the best interests of the child to resolve the issue. However, when custody challenges are between a natural parent and nonparent, the law generally has a presumption that the natural parent is the proper person to raise a child. Usually, the nonparent must show that the natural parent is not fit to raise the child. This has most often been shown by demonstrating that the parent abandoned the child or cannot properly care for the child. Still, the overriding concern is what is in the best interests of a child.

CUSTODY AND VISITATION—GENERALLY

Although federal law does impact child custody, visitation, and support in certain areas, overwhelmingly, the issue of who has custody of a child is determined by the laws of each state. The term *custody* means the right and responsibility to make decisions on behalf of a child, including those related to the child's health, education, and discipline. Traditionally, custody of a child has been granted to one parent, called the *custodial parent* (who is usually the mother), with the *noncustodial parent* (usually the father) having certain visitation rights.

Joint Custody

The notion that both parents should have more active roles and responsibilities in their children's lives led to the development of the concept of *joint custody*. There are two types of joint custody.

1. *Joint legal custody* occurs when parents share the control and responsibility for raising their child. They each have the right to participate in making major decisions about their child, and they each have access to important records concerning their child (such as school and health records). A joint legal custody arrangement may (but does not have to) include the alternating of physical custody of the child between the parents.

2. *Joint physical custody* occurs when the child lives alternately with each parent according to a *parenting schedule*. Most often, the daily decisions are made by the parent with whom the child is currently living, but major decisions (like religion, education, medical care, discipline, choice of school or camp) are jointly made.

When both parents equally share the legal and physical custody of the child, it is sometimes called *shared parenting*. Because of the degree of contact required between the parents, this type of arrangement works best where both parents are able to communicate well and are committed to resolving their differences for the sake of raising the child in a caring, nurturing environment.

Split Custody

The term *split custody* covers situations where there is more than one child and each parent has sole custody of at least one child with visitation rights for the other parent. For example, the son may live with the dad and visit his mom and sister, while the daughter may live with the mom and visit her dad and brother.

GETTING CUSTODY

Unless a court orders otherwise, when parents are married, both parents have custody. Both parents have the same rights and responsibilities to make decisions for the child.

Unwed Parents

When the parents were never married, the issue of custody and visitation is determined by law. Parental rights must be determined before a person can assert them. Therefore, the legal father of the child must be recognized by law in a *paternity* or *parentage* case. In many states, where both parents agree, parental rights may be established by filing a document, typically called an *affidavit of paternity* or *acknowledgment of parentage*. Once this form is filed, paternity is established and custody and support may then be determined.

A man who the mother claims is the father is called an *alleged father* or a *putative father* until paternity is established. If the alleged father does not agree that he is the legitimate father, the mother may file a paternity complaint against the alleged father to ask a court to determine paternity after scientific tests (usually DNA tests) are performed and evaluated. If the father wishes to legitimize his interest in his child, but the mother does not agree, the father can also file a paternity complaint, and the same tests can be made to legally determine the question of fatherhood. (See the examples of the forms used to establish paternity in Appendix A and a blank form in Appendix B.)

Unfit Parents

When parents cannot or will not properly care for the child, all states provide a procedure for another person (or the state) to get custody. This may or may not lead to adoption of a child. When a parent is determined to be unfit, the court can terminate parental rights. A termination of all parental rights and obligations includes custody, visitation, and support. While states differ in the specific factors required to be proven to terminate a parent's rights, the grounds generally include child abuse, neglect, or abandonment.

Example:

A child is brought into the emergency room of a hospital by a parent. Due to the nature of the child's injuries and other circumstances, the emergency room physician in good faith reports a belief that the child has been abused to the state's child welfare agency. To protect the child, the agency takes emergency temporary custody. An investigation confirms that child abuse did take place and one of the parents was the abuser. The state then files a case in court against that parent to protect the child and to determine the parent's fitness.

If the court finds that the child has been abused by a parent, the court has the power to take the necessary action to protect the child. This may include placing the child in foster care or with a suitable relative, ordering the parent into counseling or to take a parenting class, and even terminating all parental rights of that parent.

Psychological Parent

If a third person has established a parental bond with the child because the parent has died, disappeared, or is not interested in raising the child, this third person is sometimes referred to as a *psychological parent*. A foster parent, for example, may become the child's psychological parent.

There are two schools of thought in deciding custody between a parent and a nonparent. Most states presume that it is best for a child to be in the custody of a parent, so unless the parent is unfit or unwilling, the parent is the preferred custodian. Some courts today, however, will look at which person would provide the best environment for the child. If a child has lived with another family member or a third person and has become integrated into that home, a court may grant custody to this psychological parent where the child's interests are best served by staying in the custody of that psychological parent.

De Facto Parent

The newest category of persons who have been permitted to claim a right to seek custody or visitation with a child is called a *de facto parent*. Nearly half of the states now recognize that a nonparent caregiver may have the same rights as a parent in custody cases if that person satisfies the definition of de facto custodian.

One state defines a *de facto custodian* as the primary caregiver and financial support of a child who has lived with that person for at least six months if the child is under age 3, and one year if the child is at least age 3. After the court determines that the person is a de facto custodian, he or she has the same legal standing in custody cases as a parent, and his or her input concerning the child will be considered by the court. Custody of the child is then determined based on the best interests of the child.

For example, in May 2006, the United States Supreme Court refused to block a woman from seeking custody of a child she raised with her same-sex domestic partner in Washington. The Washington Supreme Court had determined that the woman was a de facto custodian of the seven-year-old girl. Even though the woman was not the girl's natural or adoptive mother, she functioned as a de facto parent. (*Britain v. Carvin*, 126 S. Ct. 2021 (2006).)

TAXES AND CUSTODY

The tax laws administered by the Internal Revenue Service govern the issue of taxes and custody. Currently, the parent with custody in a sole custody arrangement is entitled to the *dependency exemption* for a child. For joint custody arrangements, the exemption goes to the parent who has physical custody for the greater part of the year. In sole custody or joint custody cases, the exemption can be transferred to the other parent by agreement, and by filing a form with the IRS. The Internal Revenue Service applies the same rules to parents who have never married. Currently, the Internal Revenue Service requires Form 8332 be attached to any claim for the dependency exemption by a noncustodial parent. Because the revenue rules change periodically, check with your local IRS office for the proper form and filing requirements.

The Law of Custody and Visitation: Best Interests of the Child

When custody and visitation issues are between legal parents, courts will usually be guided by what is in the best interests of the child. When nonparents seek custody or visitation, usually the law grants parents a superior right, so the nonparent will have to show that the parent is unfit or unable to care for the child. Some jurisdictions, though, have begun to utilize the best interests standard in these cases, while giving significant weight to the right of the legal parent to custody or visitation. This is because some courts are beginning to recognize that a child has an independent right to continued contact with the person with whom the child has a parent-like relationship.

BEST INTERESTS BETWEEN PARENTS

Most states have laws that list the relevant factors to be considered in deciding what is in the best interests of the child. These factors will be discussed in more detail in the rest of the chapter. In some cases, most of the factors will weigh in favor of one parent. It is then easy for the court to decide. However, where both parents are *fit and proper* persons to have custody of their child, a court will look carefully at the relevant factors.

The fact that a court might find it to be in the best interests of a child to place custody with one parent does not necessarily mean that the other parent is not also a fit and proper parent. Nevertheless, it does mean that the court has weighed the relevant factors and found that the weight of those factors favored one parent more than the other.

FACTORS CONSIDERED

The *best interests* of the child include considering all of the parents' and child's wishes and the living circumstances that have an impact on the child's well-being. Many states define best interests in their state statutes or codes by listing the factors that will be considered.

When parents contest custody, a judge weighs the various best interest factors to decide the matter. In considering the issue of custody/visitation, courts are guided by the overriding principle that a child should be raised in a stable environment with a parent who can put the child's best interest ahead of his or her own when the two conflict.

Statutory Custody Factors Many states' laws list the following relevant factors in deciding custody:

- ✪ the wishes of the child's parent or parents as to custody;

- ✪ the wishes of the child as to his or her custodian;

- ✪ the interaction and interrelationship of the child with his or her parent or parents, siblings, and any other significant person in the child's life;

- ✪ the child's adjustment to home, school, and community;

- ✪ the mental and physical health of all the parties;

- ✪ threats or violence against, or witnessed by, the child;

- ✪ the ability of the parents to cooperate; and,

- ✪ the residential circumstances of the parents.

In addition, states may, through their individual laws or court opinions, consider other factors, such as:

- ✪ interference with the other parent's relationship with the child;

- ✪ attempting to change the child's name;

- ✪ wealth of the parents, work history, or failure to pay child support;

- ✪ work patterns of parents;

- ✪ integration of child into parent's family unit;

- ✪ age, sex, and religious considerations of the parties; and,

- ✪ cohabitation or lifestyle issues.

Generally, the relevant topics and questions that are asked in the examination of the best interests of a child include those that follow in this section through page 31.

Love and Affection   The relationship that exists between the parents and their child is one of the most important factors in determining what is in the best interests of that child. Courts want to know how a parent and child interact with one another. When the child is happy or has a problem, to whom does the child go? What has the child said on this topic? In considering the child's opinion, courts consider the child's age and maturity, reason for desire, existence of external pressure (to say or do one thing or another for one parent or against the other), and whether the child changes his or her mind (and if so, why).

Parental Care   Parental care relates to which parent can more adequately undertake the upbringing and homemaking responsibilities for a child on a daily basis. The following questions may help discover this answer.

- ✪ Who spends more hours per day with the child?

- ✪ Who cooks the meals?

- ✪ If it is a young child, who bathes and dresses the child?

- ✪ Who stays home from work when the child is sick?

- ✪ Who takes responsibility for involvement in school and who helps to complete homework assignments when needed?

- ✪ Who goes to the school conferences?

- ✪ Who attends school events?

- ✪ How does the child get to and from school activities?

- ✪ Who takes responsibility for involvement in after-school activities?

- ✪ Who is responsible for the child's religious education (if any)?

- ✪ Who makes the doctor and dentist appointments and who takes the child to these appointments?

- ✪ Who is responsible for setting up and maintaining child care arrangements?

Other Relationships   A court will also look at the significant relationships in the child's life. Are there brothers or sisters who will be affected by the custody decision? Children often wish to stay together, and the impact of any separation on them will be reviewed carefully. Also, are there new relationships in the parents' lives that will affect the child?

Economic Resources   Although courts do consider resources and economic issues, they are careful not to give too much consideration to the parent with the most assets in determining the best interests of a child. This is because both parents have a duty to support the child, so this factor can be equalized by child support, regardless of who has custody. This topic considers who pays for the child's food, clothing, medical care, or other basic needs. Who has greater earning capacity? Who has a greater likelihood of future income? Who carries (or has the ability to obtain) insurance for the child?

Guidance and Discipline

When analyzing the issue of guidance and discipline, the court will examine which parent provides the necessary correction for the child. Questions like the following are asked.

- ✪ In what manner is the child corrected?

- ✪ Who disciplines the child?

- ✪ Under what circumstances is the child disciplined and how is the discipline done or handled?

- ✪ How do the parents view each other's choice of corrective methods?

- ✪ Does each parent have the ability to separate the child's needs from his or her own needs?

- ✪ How does each parent empathize with the child?

Stability and Permanence

Stability is one of the most important factors in determining best interests. According to numerous studies, children do best when they have a stable environment. Divorce and separation can disrupt a child's relationship with his or her parents during a critical time of development, so courts weigh this factor heavily.

- ✪ Who has more flexibility to adjust working hours if needed to care for the child?

- ✪ Who has access to extended family? (Greater access to grandparents, family members, or friends who can provide care for the child is important in the issue of stability.)

- ✪ Who can provide continuity? (In the area of permanence, the court examines the length of time the child has lived in a satisfactory environment and whether that should be continued.)

Security   Courts are very concerned with the safety of a child's environment. In examining what is in the child's best interest, the court will examine each parent's past and present conduct as it relates to the child's security.

- Who can provide a safe environment?

- Has there been any verbal, physical, or sexual abuse?

- Does a parent have a substance abuse problem?

- Has a parent been arrested or convicted of a crime?

Domestic violence, whether directed at the child or witnessed by the child, is an important security issue.

- Have there been incidents of violence in the home?

- Were police called?

- Are there any threats of kidnapping?

- Has a parent ever failed to produce a child for visitation?

- Has a parent failed to appear for visitation?

- Was anyone notified?

- Has the parent ever interfered in visitation or failed to return the child at the scheduled time?

Moral Fitness   The consideration of moral fitness has been somewhat narrowed over the last several years, but the moral fitness of the parents as it relates to how they will function as parents remains important. Moral fitness sometimes overlaps with the topic of security. Covered in this category are questions of verbal and substance abuse, abuse of the child, and other illegal conduct. Also, offensive behaviors, such as a parent's questionable ethics or antisocial behavior, will be scrutinized to determine the impact on the child.

Mental and Physical Health

Physical or mental health problems that significantly interfere with the child's health and well-being are relevant in determining what is in the best interests of a child. How does the parent respond if a child needs special care? In addition, courts will examine the parents' health. Does either parent smoke, use drugs, or drink alcohol? Do they have physical or mental ailments? How will these affect the child?

Cooperation

The willingness of a parent to cooperate is extremely important to a court in deciding what is in the best interests of a child. Alienating a child from the other parent is usually viewed negatively in considering what is in the best interest of the child. Courts will also consider how conflicts have been resolved in the past. What are the parents willing to do to encourage a continuing relationship with each parent? Who is most likely to facilitate a good relationship for the child with both parents?

The wishes of the parents are given considerable weight in determining custody. However, these wishes are also weighed against whether they are in the best interest of the child.

Example:

A parent who wants custody to punish the other parent or because he or she deserves it will not have his or her wishes given much weight.

Desires of the Child and Parents

With increasing frequency, the wishes of the child is becoming an important factor in determining best interests. However, while younger children may be asked for their preference, their answers will be weighed against their age, growth, and development. For example, an 8-year-old's desire to live with mom instead of dad because mom lets him stay up later on school nights will not be given much weight, where other factors are equal. In most states, once the child reaches ages 12 to 14, his or her preference as to the custodial parent will be given greater consideration.

In cases where there is more than one child, each child may express a different preference. Experts strongly advise against splitting children, but while the law generally prefers to keep the children together, it does recognize that there are situations in which it is appropriate to separate the children. These cases may result in a form of split custody, where each parent has sole custody of at least one child, with visitation rights to the other. Split custody cases most often arise where one or more of the children are teenagers.

Example:

In a case where two brothers cannot get along, if the older one expresses a strong desire to live with his father, the court might order split custody, with the boys spending weekends together.

Keep in mind, though, that the preferences of parents and the child are not binding on the court. Generally, the weight to be given to the parents' preferences, whether to consider a child's wishes, and what weight to give those wishes, are matters left to the discretion of a trial court judge. Sometimes, courts have said they give little weight to a younger child's desires because the child was not old enough to express a real preference.

Environment   One of the most important factors in deciding what is in the best interests of a child is the child's adjustment to home, school, and his or her environment. Courts are reluctant to disrupt a child's daily living activities involving school and friends. It is important to provide consistency in living conditions, especially where young children are concerned.

Integration of the child into the home life of a parent is a critical factor in determining custody. This is one of the reasons why the status quo is so important. If, at the time of separation, one parent keeps the child in the home, the child can continue in the same school and with the same friends. A court will weigh this heavily. It favors the determination that a child has become a part of that home. The court will also be less inclined to disrupt the child's living circumstance.

Environmental concerns also involve the living conditions for a child.

Example 1:

Photographs demonstrating serious sloppiness in a mother's housekeeping were considered by a court in deciding against joint custody.

Example 2:

A father who was a doctor with a busy practice lost custody on appeal because the mother, who did not work outside the home, had a great deal more time to spend with the child. In this case, the father proposed to hire a baby-sitter when he was not present, but the court did not believe this was an acceptable alternative to the care of the other parent.

The effort to create a healthy environment for a child is extremely important in determining the best interests of a child.

Location The proposed location of the child's home is important in considering custody or visitation. The parents can be restricted from moving to a distant location under the terms of a custody or visitation agreement, or by court order.

Example:

A custodial parent may be restricted from moving to a location more than twenty-five miles from his or her present home. One (or both) parents may also be ordered to pay for transporting the child to and from one home to the other.

Religion The parent with custody is usually the person who has control over the religious upbringing of a child. Because the First Amendment guarantees religious freedom, the particular religion will only be a factor if the religious practices cause physical, emotional, or mental harm to a child.

Example:

If the demands of a certain religion interfere with the child's educational activities, a court might consider the effects of that religion on the child.

Ethnic, Cultural, Moral, and Lifestyle Issues

Ethnic, cultural, moral, and lifestyle issues can be raised in a custody proceeding, but they will only be relevant to the extent that they have an impact on the child. As the Supreme Court of Michigan explained:

> [Moral fitness], like all the other statutory factors, relates to a person's fitness as a parent. To evaluate parental fitness, courts must look to the parent-child relationship and the effect that the conduct at issue will have on that relationship. Thus, the question…is not "who is the morally superior adult"; the question concerns the parties' relatives fitness to provide for their child, given the moral disposition of each party as demonstrated by individual conduct. We hold that in making that finding, questionable conduct is relevant…only if it is a type of conduct that necessarily has a significant influence on how one will function as a parent. (Fletcher v. Fletcher, 447 Mich. 871 (1994).)

Years ago, a mother who lived with her new boyfriend (or a father who lived with his new girlfriend) might face a loss of custody. Today, that fact alone is usually not enough to establish a reason to deny custody. Instead, the court will look at the totality of the circumstances to determine whether and how the living arrangements affect the best interest of the child. Sexual activity outside the presence of the child is also often viewed to be irrelevant to the question of custody or visitation.

Example:

As the Supreme Court of Michigan has explained in the *Fletcher* case quoted above, extramarital conduct of which the children are unaware does not affect the parent's fitness.

Although lifestyle will rarely be the sole factor by which morality is judged, a parent's gay or lesbian lifestyle has sometimes been used to deny custody to a parent or to influence a decision about visitation. However, in many states, this question, like any issue of a parent's intimate relationships, will be examined for how it impacts the child's best interests.

If the child is not endangered or harmed by the relationship, the court will not likely see the relationship as a factor in its decision making. However, there are cases where the new boyfriend or girlfriend is given freedom by the parent to discipline the child, and courts have not looked positively on this aspect of such a relationship.

Race   If the parents come from different cultural or ethnic backgrounds, a court will examine this difference strictly to determine what impact it would have on the child to live in each society.

The United States Supreme Court ruled in *Palmore v. Sidoti*, 466 U.S. 429 (1984), that the race of the parent or child may not be a basis for deciding custody.

Name Change   Changing, or attempting to change, a child's name can be scrutinized by a court in determining custody. Some courts recognize that a change of a child's surname can contribute to a loss of relationship between the father and child. As one court has said:

> *A change of name imposed upon a child could represent to him a rejection by his father; or evidence that his father is deserving of rejection or contempt...or a statement by his mother and stepfather that his true identity is a shame and embarrassment to them and others. Such consequences could be enormously harmful to the child. (Mullins v. Mullins, 490 N.E.2d 1375 (Ill.App. 1986).)*

Example:
A mother who uses her new husband's name when registering a child for school or listing the child's name for activities can be harming her case for custody. Some courts view such behavior, especially where there are other indications, as part of a scheme to deprive the father of his relationship with the child.

However, other courts have allowed a child's application for a name change for more appropriate reasons.

Example:
When the reasons for a child's change to the stepfather's surname were that it would give her the same last name as her stepbrothers who attended the same school; the child expressed a love for her stepfather, but did not want to disassociate herself from her father; and, there was no misconduct by either the parents or the stepfather regarding the change, the court granted the name change, even though the father opposed the change and had consistently paid child support.

Misconduct by the Parent

The impact of misconduct by a parent on a child is an important factor in determining custody or visitation. Many types of misconduct have been considered by courts in determining what is in the best interests of a child, including:

- verbal abuse;

- drinking problems;

- lying about past alcohol abuse problems;

- a bad driving record;

- an arrest record;

- permitting a child to drink from the parent's beer;

- ✪ physical or sexual abuse of children; and,

- ✪ other illegal or offensive behaviors.

The list of misconduct is as long as the ways in which parents have engaged in negative or criminal behavior.

A parent who seeks custody or visitation should be aware that the failure to pay child support may be considered negatively on the question of custody or visitation.

Punishing a parent is not the goal of a court in determining custody or visitation. Nonetheless, substance or alcohol abuse is treated more seriously by today's courts. The problem will be considered and may operate to deprive a parent of custody or visitation, unless the parent can show that he or she has sought and received treatment, and has overcome the negative impact on the child.

Additional issues relating to kidnapping, domestic violence, child abuse, and interference with visitation are considered in Chapter 8.

FACTORS IN DECIDING VISITATION

Ordinarily, unless there are compelling reasons otherwise, when one parent is granted custody, the other will be given visitation (although the terms used may vary from state-to-state). This is because the goal of a custody/visitation proceeding is to maintain as much of the child's relationship with each parent as possible.

In deciding whether to grant visitation, courts again look to what is in the best interests of the child. For example, a history of cruelty to a child may result in a denial or significant limitation of visitation. Other negative factors include substance abuse and the inability to properly care for a child. Even in these cases, however, courts are loathe to deny visitation entirely, and may instead provide that visitation will take place under the supervision of a neutral third person. This permits the child to continue the relationship with the parent, but is designed to minimize the child's exposure to the negative parental behavior.

In granting visitation, there is no set rule on how much visitation to grant. How often the visitation will occur, and under what circumstances, depends on the particular circumstances of the parents and child. Nonetheless, to avoid problems of enforcing *reasonable* visitation rights in working out a plan for visitation, it is usually best to specify the visitation details—length, frequency, location, notice of missed visitation, etc. (See the sample visitation agreements in Appendix A.)

Geographic Location

A court may limit the geographical area where the visiting parent may take the child. This may happen when there is a real fear that the parent may take the child away from the court's jurisdiction. Of course, when one parent resides out of state, a court will normally not deny the visitation in the out-of-state location, but may require that parent to pay an amount of money to the court to be held until the child is returned to the state.

Agreement to Give Up Visitation to Avoid Child Support

One parent's agreement to give up visitation in exchange for an agreement by the other parent not to seek child support is void and will not be enforced in the courts. A parent cannot excuse the other parent from the obligation to pay child support. (For more information, see the child support chapters in this book.)

Nonparents

Because of the changing ways in which families are formed, there are many more cases today where a nonbiological parent, like a stepparent, seeks custody or visitation.

NONPARENTS AND CUSTODY

In nearly half of the states, a de facto parent can seek custody. Although the state laws differ, most direct courts to determine whether the nonparent has established a parent-child relationship, and if so, whether the parental preference has been rebutted by a showing that the parent is not acting in the best interests of the child. If both these factors exist, then the court has the power to consider whether it is in the best interests of a child to grant custody to the de facto parent.

One example of such a situation is found in the case of a man who was a de facto live-in parent to a boy from the time he was 3 years old until the boy's mother died when the boy was in his early teens. After the mother's death, the de facto parent sought custody, but so did the natural father. The court initially granted the natural father custody, but on appeal, the decision was reversed and the boy, then 14 years old, was given the opportunity to state who he wanted to live with. He chose his de facto father. The trial court later granted the natural father and the de facto father joint custody, and allowed the boy to return to live with his de facto father. (*Meldrum v. Novotny,* 640 N.W. 2d 460 (S.D. 2002).)

NONPARENTS AND VISITATION

In some states, stepparents or other persons may be entitled to visitation with the child. For example, stepparents are specifically granted the right to seek visitation by statutes in California (Cal. Family Code Ann., Sec. 3101) and Wisconsin (Wisconsin Stat. Ann., Sec. 767.245). Virginia allows not only stepparents, but also blood relatives or family members to seek visitation under certain circumstances. (Virginia Code Ann., Sec. 16.1-241(a).) Although the Supreme Court case of *Troxel v. Granville* (see below) applies to grandparent visitation, it is likely that courts will apply the same standards when determining third-party visitation issues as well.

Grandparents   In the past, grandparents have not had any right to visit their grandchildren, but legislatures and courts began to increasingly recognize the importance of this relationship for the child. Although courts must give special weight to a parent's wishes if that parent has custody, the laws of every state provide for some level of grandparent visitation when it is in the best interests of the child. Some states also allow other third parties, such as aunts and uncles, to file for visitation in certain limited circumstances.

In 2000, the United States Supreme Court, in the case of *Troxel v. Granville,* considered Washington state's grandparent visitation scheme. The Washington law allowed *any person* to seek visitation at any time, and a court could order the visitation if it was in the best interests of the child.

In *Troxel,* the paternal grandparents had regularly seen their son Brad's two girls on weekends when Brad, who lived with his parents, had visitation. Brad died, and for several months more, the grandparents continued to have visitation on the same weekend schedule. However, the mother remarried and decided to limit the grandparents to seeing the girls just one time per month. The grandparents went to court to expand their visitation, but the United States Supreme Court decided that the "any person-any time" language of the statute was invalid, because it failed to give special consideration to the mother's wishes. The Supreme Court said as long as a parent is fit to have custody, special weight must be given to that parent's decision concerning visitation.

As a result of this decision, some states have changed their laws on visitation. For example, in construing *Troxel*, an appellate court in Texas decided that grandparents must overcome a presumption that a parent who is otherwise fit acts in the best interests of his or her child. A grandparent, under the law, must show that denial of visitation works a significant impairment of the child's physical or emotional well-being.

After *Troxel*, many states have made changes to their grandparent laws. Alabama passed a law that grandparents have a right to file for visitation, even if there is no divorce pending, where a parent has denied the grandparent a relationship with the child. (ALA. Code, Sec. 30-3-4.1.) Arizona law grants great-grandparents the same rights as grandparents to petition for visitation. (Ariz.Rev. Stat. Sec. 25-409.)

Perhaps the strongest statement on grandparents became law in 2004 in New York. There the legislature recognized that there are 413,000 children living in grandparent-headed households, and that grandparents play a special role in the lives of their grandchildren. New York provides special guidance regarding the ability of grandparents to file for custody of their grandchildren in extraordinary circumstances.

Oklahoma requires a showing of parental unfitness or a showing that a child would suffer potential harm without grandparent visitation, and sets out specific factors that must now be considered. (Okla. Stat. tit. 10, Sec. 2001.) However, in North Carolina, a court ruled that if the grandparent cannot show that a grandchild was the subject of a custody proceeding, the grandparent cannot seek visitation rights.

If this is an issue in your case, be sure to check for the most current law in this area. Review the discussion in Chapter 1 on "Legal Research" to help you find the most current supplement or pocket update of the law for your state.

Developing Your Parenting Plan

Children often suffer when they are the subject of protracted custody disputes. One useful resource for children is "A Kid's Guide to Divorce," which can be found online at **www.kidshealth.org**. Lengthy proceedings are also emotionally and financially taxing to the parents. When the parents can agree on custody, it reduces the toll that these proceedings take on the child and encourages the parents to cooperate in raising their child. Parents who agree on the terms of a custody arrangement are also more likely to abide by the custody order. The agreement can operate to reduce later conflict between the parents. Finally, expenses saved on the litigation costs can be used more productively towards family expenses.

While a court is not required to accept the parents' agreement concerning custody and visitation, it usually will if the agreement is reasonable and not contrary to the best interests of the child. Without an agreement, it is up to the judge to make the ultimate decision about what is in the best interest of the child. The risk, of course, is that the judge's decision may be based on the preferences of the judge instead of the desires of the parents.

Example:
In a study on judicial attitudes in making custody decisions, it was determined that judges preferred an arrangement where the child spent the school year with one parent and had summer vacation with the other.

Leaving the decision of custody up to the preference of a judge may not reflect what you as the parents—who have the greatest investment in the future welfare of your child—believe to be in the best interests of your child.

FORMULATING AN AGREEMENT

Custody and visitation agreements may be very short or very long and detailed documents, depending on the parents' personalities and desires. Most agreements fall somewhere in between. It is also true that the less cooperation between the parents, the more detailed the agreement should be to avoid *interpretation* problems. Ideally, a custody/visitation agreement should be detailed enough to avoid complaints, but flexible enough to accommodate inevitable changes over the course of several years.

NOTE: *Remember that once the agreement is included in a court judgment, it becomes binding until you return to court and get it modified, unless you provide otherwise.*

For a sample completed custody and visitation agreement, see the sample, filled-in **PARENTING PLAN** in Appendix A on page 187. To create your own **PARENTING PLAN**, see the forms in Appendix B. (see form 12, p.228 and form 13, p.234.)

Agreement to Cooperate

An *agreement to cooperate* provision is a general statement of the intent of you and the other parent to cooperate for the benefit of your child. It is not a formal requirement that you or the other parent do something, but serves as a reminder to both of you that your primary concern should be your child.

Custody   The custody provision describes the custody arrangement, usually in the terms used in your state's law. Depending upon the state, there may be a distinction between *legal custody* (or decision-making custody) and *physical custody* (regarding where the child lives a majority of the time). Also, the terminology used may vary by state. For example, Florida law refers to *parental responsibility* and *primary residence*, whereas Texas law refers to *managing conservatorship*.

Visitation   In the past, many agreements or court orders referred simply to *reasonable visitation*—but what exactly does *reasonable* mean? Ask a few people and you will get a few different answers. That is why most agreements should provide a greater level of detail. See the sample **PARENTING PLAN** forms in Appendix A. Consider the following in preparing your plan.

- ✪ When can the parent visit? Which days, holidays, or vacation times are best?

- ✪ What should the frequency of visitation be (every weekend, every other weekend)?

- ✪ How will you handle visitation for summer vacations, winter vacations, spring vacations, and holidays?

- ✪ What holidays and other special occasions are to be included? (Typical days of importance include New Year's Eve and New Year's Day, Good Friday, Passover, Easter, Memorial Day weekend, July Fourth weekend, Rosh Hashanah, Yom Kippur, Thanksgiving, Christmas Eve, Christmas Day, the child's and parents' birthdays, Mother's Day, Father's Day, school holidays, and any other days of significance within your family (e.g., anniversaries, grandparents' birthdays, etc.).)

- ✪ What times should the child be picked up and returned?

- ✪ Who is responsible for bringing the child and returning the child from the visitation location, and who pays the transportation costs?

The possibilities are as varied as are the schedules and geographic factors of the parents.

Example:

Parents who live around the corner from one another may share significant time with the child, but for a parent who lives in another city or state, visitation may need to be more limited.

NOTE: *Put each of these detailed sections in its own paragraph, identified by a number or letter. That way, any disagreements will be easier to resolve, because the issue can be narrowed to a specific, identifiable section of the parenting agreement.*

Education   Your agreement should include provisions relating to your child's education. You may agree to send your child to public or private school. You may also cover the issues of a change of school or special classes. Decisions regarding continuing education after high school may also be addressed.

Notices and Information   There are various types of notices and information from schools, health care providers, and others that are normally provided or available to parents regarding their children. These include such things as report cards, test results, school field trip information and permission slips, reminders of doctor and dentist appointments, and medical records. When one parent has custody, such information is typically sent, or made available, to that parent. You may agree that such information will be given by the parent who normally receives it to the other parent, or that each parent will have direct access to the information. You should consider the following questions.

- Who should be contacted if the child gets sick or has a serious illness or injury?

- Who should have access to the child's medical records?

- Who should have access to information about the child's progress at school?

Contacting the Other Parent

Obviously, it is extremely important that parents share information about how they can be contacted by each other. Your agreement may include a provision that you will each keep the other informed of any changes in address or telephone numbers.

Travel

Many families include travel in their vacation plans, and the custody/visitation agreement should cover this issue also.

- ✪ May the parent with custody or the visiting parent take the child on trips?

- ✪ If so, for how long?

- ✪ During what periods of time?

- ✪ To what destinations? Out of state? Out of the country? To certain foreign countries, but not others?

- ✪ What type and amount of advance notice must be given to the other parent?

- ✪ If the parent with custody takes the child on a trip and it interferes with visitation, or if the visiting parent takes the child on a trip and it interferes with the other parent's time with the child, how will this be handled? (Makeup time?)

Changes in Visitation Schedule

Some degree of flexibility should be built into the visitation schedule, because it is common that some changes will occasionally need to take place. Special events or emergencies can occur that may make a change desirable or necessary.

- ✪ If the visiting parent wants to change the time or day of visitation, how much notice should be given and how will it be communicated? (Phone call, email, etc.)

- ✪ How much advance notice should be given if additional visiting time is desired?

- ✪ How much advance notice should be given if the visiting parent will not be able to visit as scheduled?

- ✪ What happens if the visiting parent does not visit as agreed?

Moving   Moving is a common occurrence in this highly mobile world. The laws and rules regarding moving vary from state to state. States have the power to regulate relocation, either by statute—as in Illinois, Massachusetts, and New Jersey—or through their inherent power over the parents. Most states, like Colorado and Florida, generally permit relocation if the planned move is in the best interests of the child, while New York has moved away from requiring a parent to show exceptional circumstances to whether a move will be in the best interests of a child.

Recently, more states are willing to look at all the circumstances presented by the proposed move to see whether it is in the best interests of the child. Most often, agreements address this issue and place a restriction on moving. In some states, any agreement (which is incorporated into the order or judgment) must contain a provision that the child shall not be removed from the state unless by agreement of the parties or with the approval of a judge. You must consider what happens if a parent wishes to move.

In evaluating a proposed relocation plan, you might consider the following.

- ✪ Is the move in the best interests of the child?

- ✪ What is the motive?

- ✪ Will the out-of-state custodial parent be likely to comply with the visitation order?

- ✪ Will this visitation be adequate to foster a continuing meaningful relationship between the children and the noncustodial parent?

- ✪ What is the cost of transportation? Who will pay it?

Violations   Sadly, violations of custody or visitation agreements are common. This partly stems from the acrimony that sometimes accompanies the entry of the original custody or visitation order, or a belief by a party that his or her rights are being abridged. This party may feel justified in retaliatory violations to the point where violations become the defining behavior of the agreement.

Resolving Disputes

There are many reasons for not going back to see a judge every time you and the other parent have a dispute regarding visitation. Going to court can be expensive and time-consuming, and it can take some time to get a hearing scheduled. Therefore, you may want to put a provision in your agreement to attempt to resolve problems through some type of *alternative dispute resolution.*

Examples of alternative dispute resolution include seeing a counselor or going through mediation, where a trained, neutral third party tries to help you and the other parent work out a settlement. Although not every problem should be the subject of alternative dispute resolution, you can agree to use this much less expensive alternative to try to settle any disagreements that may arise.

The question of how to resolve these problems and how the costs of alternative dispute resolution will be paid may be addressed in the custody/visitation agreement. If alternative dispute resolution does not work or is not suitable for the problem, there are still court proceedings available to enforce or change the agreement if necessary.

Visitation with Others

If you agree that another family member (or anyone else) should have visitation with your child, it should be specifically stated in your agreement.

JOINT CUSTODY

Joint custody arrangements became popular in the 1970s. At the beginning, it was thought that this would be the solution to contested custody cases. However, in the years that followed, it became clear that joint custody is not the best alternative for every case, because it requires both parents to be willing to compromise self-interest for the the best interest of the child.

Joint custody requires extensive contact and intensive communication between parents. It does not work well in situations where the parties have a lot of hostility or manipulate the child for their own ends. Because of this, some states have strict statutory guidelines that must be met for a joint custody order. Also, in some states, before a court can grant joint custody, the parties must have agreed, in writing, to the terms of the joint custody (sometimes called a *joint parenting agreement*).

Joint Custody Factors

If you are considering joint custody, you should evaluate:

- ✪ whether you believe joint custody would be the best choice;

- ✪ whether you can communicate well with each other;

- ✪ whether you agree to share decision-making responsibilities;

- ✪ whether you both live reasonably close to each other in order to avoid disrupting your child's school, home, and friends;

- ✪ whether both of your home environments make it easy to take your child back and forth;

- ✪ whether your work schedules and routines accommodate your child's needs; and,

- ✪ how your child feels about joint custody.

JOINT PARENTING AGREEMENTS

A joint parenting agreement is basically the same as a custody/visitation agreement, except that it has some provisions that are unique to the joint custody situation. For example, a joint parenting agreement will have the same types of provisions that were discussed in the previous section of this chapter. The following are some comments on matters that should be included in a joint parenting agreement.

Agreement to Cooperate

The *agreement to cooperate* provision discussed on page 36 should also be included in any joint custody arrangement. In addition, it is common to see more than one paragraph that expresses a desire to work together for the benefit of the child.

Parenting Time

Even though the joint parenting agreement forces a high degree of cooperation, it is still important to set forth the time that each parent will be responsible for the child. Like an agreement for custody and visitation, the parents should set out provisions for where the child will be on holidays, significant days, and vacations to avoid a potential disagreement. The main difference is that you will replace the terms *custody* and *visitation* with other terms, such as *parenting time*. It is also important to address for what each parent is responsible (activities, issues, checkups, etc.) during the time the child lives with him or her and during the transition times.

Location of Parents' Residences

For a joint parenting arrangement (where the child spends significant time with each parent) to really work, it is ideal if the parents live in close proximity to one another. It is common to agree to a geographic distance within which they will live while the child grows. A paragraph on this topic would set forth why this is important and exactly what the parties agree is the maximum distance.

Moving

If a parent desires to move during the term of the agreement, the parties would have to renegotiate the terms of the joint custody agreement to where each saw the child frequently, because close proximity is such a big part of the agreement. To do this, the parents could work out another joint parenting agreement or a sole custody/visitation arrangement and file the modification with the court for approval. (See Chapter 12 on modification of custody and visitation orders.)

Remarriage

The joint parenting agreement will be designed to be effective regardless of the remarriage of one of the parents. It is helpful, though, to place such a paragraph in your agreement in order to clarify that you both recognize this.

Dispute Resolution

Studies show that when parties with joint parenting agreements work out their differences without having to turn to a court, they express a much greater overall satisfaction with the agreement and are more willing to follow it. Perhaps this is because, while we cannot always get what we want, we can always listen to the other person and be heard ourselves. This is the function of mediation—keeping the lines of communication open. Remember, the parenting responsibility that you both have agreed to share will last throughout your child's youth.

Custody and Visitation Checklist of Factors to Consider

TOPIC	MOTHER	FATHER

Time spent with a parent (before and after separation)
    Hours per day?
    How is time spent?
    How is substitute care arranged?		

Parental care
    Meals: purchase/preparation?
    Clothing purchase/dressing of child?
    School-related (conferences, transportation)?
    Child's outside activities?
    Medical and dental care?
    Child's special needs?
    Who works outside the home?
    Who can adjust work if child is sick or needy?		

Discipline
    Who is responsible?
    Kind of discipline used?		

Love and affection between parent and child
    How is love shown?
    Child more affectionate with?
    Child's preference?		

Guidance
    Who is more likely to provide?
    Who does child go to for help?
    Who does child tell of successes?
    Child's home and school performance while
        under guidance of parent?		

TOPIC	MOTHER	FATHER

Security
    Who can provide safe environment for child?
    Mental and physical health?
    Abuse of child or other parent?
    Substance abuse?
    Arrest record?
    Driving record?
    General fitness of parent?		

Stability
    Who can put child's needs ahead of their own?
    Who is more cooperative?
    Who has access to extended family support?
    How long has parent lived in residence?
    Past pattern of moves?
    Future intent to move?		

Permanence
    Who has greater earnings?
    Capacity for future earnings?
    Who provides insurance for child?
    Ages?
    If there has been a trial period, how have parties
    handled:
        transportation?
        visitation?		

Other relationships that have an impact on the child
    Adults?
    Other children?		

Filing Your Case

Now that you have considered your options and have possibly begun working out an arrangement, you are ready to start the process of filing for custody or visitation. You may be filing for custody or visitation as part of your divorce case or as an independent case. The forms in Appendix B will be helpful. The explanations in this chapter provide information on the custody or visitation portions of the case. Later chapters on child support will explain the support sections of your case.

This chapter is designed to make you an informed participant in the legal system in the area of child custody and visitation. However, if you are not able to communicate with the other parent, and you believe that the other parent will contest custody, you are well-advised to seek a consultation with a lawyer before you proceed in court. (The role of the lawyer was discussed in Chapter 1.) Like any other resource, a legal professional can help you sort through your state's specific laws and nuances, so that you can proceed with the best information available.

PREPARATION FOR YOUR CASE

Once you have considered your options, and where appropriate, discussed them with the other parent, you are ready to begin preparing your case. Even if you and the other parent have agreed to all of the terms regarding custody and visitation, you will still need to gather certain information to put into the documents you must eventually file with the court. If you have not agreed, or believe you may not be able to agree, this information and the documents discussed below will be essential for you to prove your case.

In preparing to file your custody or visitation case, you must gather certain information about yourself, your child, and the other parent. Because the issues of custody and visitation are bound together with the issue of child support, much of the information and documents you will need are financial in nature. The financial information you will need to gather is discussed in detail in Chapter 11. The following sections describe the nonfinancial areas in which you will need to collect information while preparing your case.

PARENTAL INFORMATION

In addition to the financial information discussed in Chapter 11, you will need basic information about you and your spouse, such as:

- ✪ your full name, birth date, Social Security number, and current home and business addresses and phone numbers;

- ✪ the other parent's full name, birth date, Social Security number, and current home and business addresses and phone number;

- ✪ employment information for you and the other parent, especially information about employment hours and travel requirements. In a custody dispute, this may be important to show the relative time each of you has available to be with the child, especially at vital times, such as when the child gets home from school and in the evening. In visitation, this may be important to setting up a visitation schedule. (You will also need financial information about employment, which will be discussed in detail in Chapter 11.);

✪ information about your and the other parent's health. (If the other parent has a medical condition that may affect his or her ability to care for your child, obtain the name and office address of the other parent's doctor); and,

✪ who else lives in each of your households. (This may have a bearing on issues such as who else might be available to help care for your child, whether there is adequate space in your home, and how the child might get along with other household members.)

INFORMATION ABOUT YOUR CHILD

The type of information you will need about your child will depend somewhat upon the issues that are raised in your case. The following information and questions should be considered. Some of what is listed will be needed in your case and some are things to consider simply for the benefit of your child. You will also need information about finances that relate to your child; however, as this relates more directly to child support, it is discussed in detail in Chapter 11.

Typical information includes:

✪ the full name, age, date of birth, and Social Security number of each child;

✪ information about any mental or physical condition or illness of the child (disabilities, special requirements, the name and address of your child's doctor, etc.);

✪ school information about the child;

✪ with whom your child now resides, for how long this arrangement has existed, and the living arrangements prior to the separation of the parents;

✪ any previous custody orders relating to your child and any copies of them;

- ✪ whether you have spoken to your child about custody, about the other parent (or yourself) visiting with your child, how the child responded to these questions, whether he or she expressed any preferences, and what your child's attitude is and why the child has this attitude; and,

- ✪ what your plans are for vacations.

GATHERING AND SAVING THE DOCUMENTS

Gather copies of any documents that contain important information to use later in your case. Keep the documents in a safe place and periodically update the documents with more current information. Also, keep up the daily log that you began writing during the custody and visitation tryout period. Even if there is no tryout period, a log will help you see what responsibilities you undertook to care for your child during the time you kept the log. Also, write down problems, issues, and unusual expenses, along with the date, time, place, and names of any persons who were present. When you are ready to take the next step of filing your case in court, you will find that much of the information you will need will be available at your fingertips.

WHO CAN FILE

Only a person with the legal right to do so may file for custody. State law will determine who has such a right. In all states, either the child's mother or father can file for custody or visitation. If the parents are married to each other, the issues of custody and visitation will be addressed as part of a case for divorce (in some states, this may be called a *dissolution of marriage*), legal separation, or annulment. If the parents are not married to each other, a separate lawsuit for custody or visitation may be filed.

If permitted by state law, certain persons who are not parents may also file for custody. This may include grandparents, aunts, uncles, or anyone else. In addition, all states have laws permitting some form of grandparent visitation, so a grandparent may file for visitation.

WHAT YOU MUST PROVE

In a case seeking a determination of child custody or visitation, the petitioner (the person who files the petition) must prove, by a *preponderance of the evidence* (meaning at least a 51% probability), that it is in the best interests of the child to follow the custody or visitation request as requested in the petition.

WHERE TO FILE

Explaining where to file your case requires a short explanation of the legal terms *jurisdiction* and *venue*. Jurisdiction means that a court has the power to hear a custody case. Venue refers to the actual physical location of the court that will decide the custody suit.

Example:

The State of California will have jurisdiction for parents who live with their child in San Diego, California; however, the courts of San Diego will be the proper venue within which to file the suit for custody.

You will file your documents with the clerk of the court. The clerk's office is responsible for accepting documents, collecting the fees for filing, and maintaining the files. Remember that there will usually be fees due, unless you can show that you qualify for exemption by virtue of your poverty status. Check with your clerk's office for exact information on filing fees and supporting documents required to be filed. If you believe you qualify, check on how to file the necessary forms to avoid paying the filing fees. Also, ask how many copies of each form they require. Bring two extra copies so that they can be stamped with the filing date and the case number. One such copy may need to be delivered to the local sheriff's office to be served on the other parent, and you will want to keep a copy for yourself.

Uniform Child Custody Jurisdiction Act

Determining where to file is made more difficult when both parents do not live in the same state. The *Uniform Child Custody Jurisdiction Act* (UCCJA) was passed to give guidance on where to file a custody case when the parties live in different states. This law is extremely important because it effectively eliminates the problems that arise when more than one court has jurisdiction, which can cause contradictory court orders that are impossible to enforce. While the UCCJA was a significant improvement in avoiding contradictory court orders, there remained some problems in enforcement.

Uniform Child Custody Jurisdiction and Enforcement Act

More recently, the *Uniform Child Custody Jurisdiction Enforcement Act* (UCCJEA) was written to make interstate custody orders more uniform and to improve enforcement. Almost every state, as well as the U.S. Virgin Islands, has adopted the UCCJEA. Once a state adopts the UCCJEA, it will replace the UCCJA. The UCCJEA was drafted to make it clear that one state has child custody jurisdiction so that states can improve their ability to efficiently enforce custody orders. The UCCJEA gives a priority to the home state instead of the state with a significant connection. The home state keeps jurisdiction to make continuing orders as necessary. The UCCJEA also has provisions for enforcement of custody and visitation orders.

As you might expect, there are many cases filed and fought over the question of which court has the proper jurisdiction in cases in which the parents reside in different states. These cases have produced a confusing body of law, and further discussion of this issue is beyond the scope of this book. If you get involved in a situation where this type of dispute arises, you need to get a lawyer.

WHAT TO FILE

A custody or visitation case is commenced by filing a *petition* or *complaint* with the proper court. (see form 1, p.201.) (To simplify matters, the term *petition* will be used in this book.) If a petition for divorce, legal separation, or annulment is filed, it will include the matters of custody and visitation. If the parents are not married to each other, or if a nonparent seeks custody or visitation, a petition for custody or visitation will be filed.

Summons

In either situation, there will also be a form called a **SUMMONS**, which will be delivered to (the legal term is *served on*) the other parent, along with the petition, in a manner required by the law of your state.

(see form 2, p.206.) The most common method is to have these papers personally delivered to the other parent by a sheriff's deputy.

Establishing Paternity

Remember that in most states, a father who never married the mother must establish that he is the legal father of the child in order to be entitled to custody or visitation. This usually requires either that both parents sign and file a document (typically called an *acknowledgment of parentage* or an *acknowledgment of paternity*), or that the court is asked to determine who is the child's father. Having the court determine this may be done either through a *paternity* or *parentage* court proceeding filed before the petition for custody or visitation is filed, or as a part of the petition for custody or visitation.

Other Forms

There may be additional forms required by your court, so always check with the local court clerk's office for specific information. Many court clerks' offices now list some basic pleading forms on the Internet that are printable or downloadable. It may also help to request to see a few files that are pending. Go to your local clerk's office and ask to see these public files. You will usually be able to view the files at the office. You may also be able to make copies of documents. Ask the clerk for blank forms of documents that are court-generated. Some of the more common forms will be discussed later in this book.

The Parties

Whoever files the petition is usually called the *petitioner* (if a petition is filed) or the *plaintiff* (if a complaint is filed). The person the petition is filed against is commonly called the *respondent* (in a petition) or the *defendant* (in a complaint).

FILING FEES AND OTHER COSTS

There are filing fees for cases seeking to establish parentage, parenting time (custody/visitation), and child support. The clerk's office has a schedule of fees and will be able to provide you with specific filing fee information for the type of case you are going to be filing. The clerk's office can also tell you the accepted methods of payment of the fees. For example, some courts may not accept personal checks.

Fees will vary from state to state, and possibly even from county-to-county. For example, the fee for filing a custody case is $171 in Arizona, about $190 in Texas, and up to $280 in Illinois.

Other Court Clerk Fees

Some states also charge other miscellaneous fees, such as for the preparation and issuance of subpoenas, a judgment fee, a court reporter's fee, photocopying charges, and a fee to certify orders and judgments.

Service Fees

There are also separate fees (and possibly mileage costs), typically charged by the sheriff's office, for the service of the complaint and **SUMMONS**, and the service of subpoenas or other notices.

If You Cannot Afford Court Fees and Costs

If you do not have funds to pay filing and service fees, check with your clerk's office for a form to request a waiver or deferral of payment. Usually, a waiver of the fees is available only to those with a very low income. Deferral of payment allows you to pay the fees in installments or at a later time. You may also be able to request in your complaint or petition that the other party be ordered to pay some or all of these fees.

THE PETITION FOR CUSTODY OR VISITATION

The **PETITION TO ESTABLISH PATERNITY, CUSTODY AND TIME-SHARING, AND FOR CHILD SUPPORT (PETITION FOR CUSTODY)** (form 1, p.201) is designed to cover most of the matters that may arise in a custody case. You may need to change the wording to comply with local custom or eliminate portions that do not apply to your situation. Still, this form should give you a good start.

While all states' court systems may not have the same look to their documents, they cover the same basic information. For example, the court in the sample on the next page is called a *circuit* court. In another jurisdiction, this level of court might be called by a different name, such as a *superior* court, *family* court, *county* court, or *district* court. In order to find out how your court is designated, check with your local clerk or review a custody case file in the local clerk's office.

To organize and keep track of documents filed in court, all cases are assigned numbers that appear on the face of all documents filed in that case. The case number will be assigned by the clerk's office at the time you file your **PETITION FOR CUSTODY**. Therefore, you will leave the case number line blank on your **PETITION FOR CUSTODY**. The clerk will write or stamp the number on the face of the **PETITION FOR CUSTODY** when it is accepted for filing. Thereafter, you will type in the case number on all of the documents you file.

Notice that the sample below has the name of the court and its location, a place for the parties' names and a case number, and a title of the document. This portion of a legal form is called the *caption* or *case style*. Whatever the specific format, the caption to your case will include the same basic information to identify your case and the court.

IN THE CIRCUIT COURT FOR THE
TWELFTH JUDICIAL CIRCUIT
DIVORCE COUNTY, STATE OF BLISS

IN RE THE PETITION OF)
Jane Doe,)
               Petitioner,)
)
    v.)   No. _____
John Doe,)
               Respondent.)

PETITION FOR CUSTODY/VISITATION

The above example is titled a *petition*; however, in some states, this document may be called a *complaint*. Once again, check your local court rules before filling out the forms, in order to determine exactly what you should title your initial document.

The **Petition for Custody** generally includes basic information about both parents (such as names and addresses) and the child (such as name, address, birth date, age), and tells the court for what you are asking (establishing paternity, custody, visitation, or child support). At a minimum, your **Petition for Custody** should include:

- ✪ your name and address;

- ✪ the other parent's name and address;

- ✪ the child's name, address, date of birth, and age;

- ✪ the relationship of the parties to each other;

- ✪ information to show that the court has jurisdiction (this is usually information showing that a residency requirement has been met and that the child has a sufficient connection with the state); and,

- ✪ a statement as to what you want the court to do (such as establish paternity, or grant custody, visitation, or child support).

A **Petition for Custody** may also include requests for additional remedies. For example, in a divorce action, the petitioner may also be seeking *alimony* (sometimes called *maintenance*) and a division of property. In a custody case where the parties never married, one of the paragraphs is going to allege that the male party is the father of the child. Whether there is a marriage or not, child support will also be a subject of the case. The petitioner will also be required to sign the petition and verify that, to the best of his or her knowledge, the facts within it are true.

The degree of formality with which this information is customarily presented may vary from court to court. For example, in some states, a **Petition for Custody** may begin with a statement in very simple English, like the following.

| The Petitioner alleges as follows: |

However, in another state, it may be customary to use more traditionally formal language.

> Comes now Jane Doe, the Petitioner in the above entitled action, and for her Petition against John Doe, the Respondent, hereby alleges and avers as follows:

You may be able to use the first version even if most of the lawyers in your area use the second version. However, you may run into difficulty having the court clerk accept your **PETITION FOR CUSTODY**. (see form 1, p.201.) This is one reason it is important to research the format of the forms used in your court. Your research should include looking at the local court rules, checking for form and practice books at a law library, looking at files from other cases at the clerk's office, and asking if there are any standard forms that can be provided by the clerk. Try to match the local format and language as much as possible.

Other Documents

Depending on your state, other forms may be required upon filing the **PETITION FOR CUSTODY**. Some states require a form attesting that no other court has jurisdiction under the *Uniform Child Custody Jurisdiction Act* or the *Uniform Child Custody Jurisdiction and Enforcement Act* (see form 4, p.209), or require a financial information form be filed to determine child support issues.

THE SUMMONS AND SERVICE

A summons is designed to notify a person that he or she is being sued. Because the **PETITION TO ESTABLISH PATERNITY, CUSTODY AND TIME-SHARING, AND FOR CHILD SUPPORT (PETITION FOR CUSTODY)** (form 1) must accompany the summons, the respondent will also know why he or she is being sued. Although a sample **SUMMONS** is included in this book, every jurisdiction has its own summons form, so make sure you use the form that is right for the court in your area. (see form 2, p.206.)

If the parents have agreed to the terms of custody, the respondent can waive service of the summons. Otherwise, the **SUMMONS** and **PETITION FOR CUSTODY** must be served on the respondent.

Usually, the local sheriff will serve the summons, but you must find out how to arrange this. When you file your **PETITION FOR CUSTODY**, ask the clerk how service arrangements are made. In some states, the clerk will take a copy of the **PETITION FOR CUSTODY** and **SUMMONS** from you and send it automatically. In other states, there is a box or a bin in which to leave your **SUMMONS** and **PETITION FOR CUSTODY**. In still other states, it will be up to you to take a copy of the **PETITION FOR CUSTODY** and **SUMMONS** to the sheriff's office. The sheriff's office is often either within or near the court building, so you can walk there once your documents are filed.

Unless you have been previously exempted from paying fees, there will be a fee due to the sheriff or other agency that will serve the documents on the respondent. Make sure you find out how much it costs (when you talk to the clerk about filing) and bring sufficient funds.

If the respondent lives in another state, get the address of the local sheriff in the county where the respondent lives. Send the file-stamped **PETITION FOR CUSTODY** and **SUMMONS** (along with a check for the correct amount) to the proper office and request that the respondent be served there.

A summons may be served on the respondent in person to the locations that you put on the face of the summons (usually work or home). Make sure you put times when the respondent is likely to be at the specified location (such as work hours), so that the sheriff will not waste time trying to find the respondent.

When the respondent has been served, the sheriff will file what is usually called a *return of service, affidavit of service,* or a similarly named document, which explains the details of how the **SUMMONS** and **PETITION FOR CUSTODY** were served. As the petitioner, you should get a notice of this from the sheriff's office, but if some time passes and you do not hear from them, you can always check your court file at the clerk's office to see if the sheriff's return of service has been filed.

Once the respondent has been served, he or she will have a few weeks to respond to the **PETITION FOR CUSTODY**. The exact number of days depends on the jurisdiction, and will be listed in the notices section on the **Summons** form. Knowing the date of service means you can compute how long the respondent has to file an answer to the **Petition for Custody**. This will dictate your next move.

If the sheriff tries but cannot find the respondent at the location you listed, the sheriff will indicate in the return of service document that the **Summons** could not be served. If you learn or know of another address at which the respondent may be found, you will have to prepare another **Summons** with the new location information. You will then have it issued by the clerk and pay the fees a second time to have it served.

If you do not know where the respondent is, the law permits a form of notice called *service by publication*. A notice of your pending lawsuit is published in a newspaper. This is considered giving notice to the world—including the respondent. The rules for service by publication are different in each state, so check your laws carefully to learn the requirements for this form of notice.

Serving notice by publication usually requires court approval, and therefore, the filing of a motion requesting permission to serve the respondent by publication. Generally, your motion must include information about what steps you took to search for the respondent. This is called a *due diligence* requirement.

Once the court grants you permission, find out which newspapers are approved to publish notice of lawsuits. Take your publication notice (often called a *notice of action*) to the newspaper, and pay the fee the newspaper charges to publish your notice. The notice will usually appear in the newspaper several times—the exact number of times and the timing being determined by the law of your state. When it first appears, the newspaper should provide you with a clipping. If not, get a copy of the newspaper and check to see that the notice has been accurately printed. Notify the newspaper immediately if there are any errors.

RESPONDING TO A PETITION FOR CUSTODY OR VISITATION

If both parents have worked out an agreement on custody and visitation (and any other issues in the **PETITION FOR CUSTODY**), the issue of the respondent's response will be resolved when the agreement is presented for court approval.

Filing a Response

If, however, the parents have not completely agreed to all the issues raised in the **PETITION FOR CUSTODY**, it is considered a contested case. Once the respondent is served with the **SUMMONS** and **PETITION FOR CUSTODY**, he or she will have an opportunity to file a *response* (sometimes called an *answer*) to the petition. Like all documents filed in the case, the **RESPONSE TO PETITION TO ESTABLISH PATERNITY, CUSTODY AND TIME-SHARING, AND FOR CHILD SUPPORT (RESPONSE)** will have a caption and will answer each of the allegations in the **PETITION FOR CUSTODY**. (see form 3, p.207.)

Failure to Respond

If you are served with a **SUMMONS** and **PETITION FOR CUSTODY**, you should not ignore them. If you fail to respond within the time limit set by your state (as stated in the **SUMMONS**), the relief sought in the **PETITION FOR CUSTODY** may be granted, and you will not have an opportunity to contest the allegations. In your **RESPONSE**, you may choose to raise new claims (for example, your own request for custody). Usually in your **RESPONSE** you may admit, deny, or state that you have insufficient information upon which to base an answer.

If a respondent simply ignores the **PETITION FOR CUSTODY**, then upon the lapse of time within which the respondent had to file a **RESPONSE** (determined by your state's law), the petitioner can file a motion with the court to declare the respondent to be in *default*. Once the respondent is defaulted (either by court order or by a docket entry of the clerk), the court can act on the requests in your **PETITION FOR CUSTODY**.

TEMPORARY CUSTODY OR VISITATION

Once the case has been filed, the court has jurisdiction to award temporary custody, visitation, and support. These temporary orders grant rights and responsibilities until the case is resolved. The person requesting the temporary order must do so by filing a **MOTION FOR**

TEMPORARY RELIEF. (see form 7, p.215.) Depending upon the state, this may be called a *motion for temporary custody and support*, or some similar name.

If the judge grants your request, you will usually need to prepare an **ORDER FOR TEMPORARY RELIEF** (see form 10, p.225) to reflect exactly what the judge orders. Forms 7 and 10 are designed to include the various matters that may be the subject of temporary orders. You may need to modify these forms to fit the requirements of your court or your circumstances.

Remember, in filing a **MOTION FOR TEMPORARY RELIEF** with the court, you must also notify the respondent (unless he or she has been defaulted). However, you only needed to use a **SUMMONS** form at the beginning of the case. Once the respondent has been served with the **SUMMONS** and **PETITION FOR CUSTODY**, any subsequent notices or copies of court documents may be sent by mail or by other means allowed by the court rules of your state.

THE NEXT STEP

Now that the **PETITION** is pending and the court may have made some preliminary orders, the parties may be directed to *mandatory mediation*, the preferred method of resolving family law cases. Even if mediation is not mandatory, it will be an option for the parties. (See Chapter 6 for more on mediation.)

When parties cannot agree, the court must make the decision for them. This means that the case will be resolved after a trial. Relatively few cases go to trial, and most are eventually settled by the parties. (See Chapter 7 for more information on the contested custody case.)

Resolving Your Case Without a Trial: Mediation

Now that you understand something about the laws governing custody and visitation, you can begin to think about your options. As a preliminary matter, you should ask and answer the question, "What do I want?"

Upon first reflection, you might answer, "To win sole custody, of course!" However, such a win will cause you increased financial, physical, and emotional responsibilities. You will not be able to just leave and go out at any time. Being a child's sole caretaker means that you make all the decisions—the easy ones, the hard ones, and the scary ones—by yourself. This includes arranging all the details for the child's care if you travel or any time you simply need free for yourself.

On the other hand, you might think, *Well, I want to have the best of it—to visit the child whenever I want and have few or no burdens of rearing a child.* However, without actively participating in your child's life, you may become little more than another playmate, or simply a source of money or entertainment—buying your child instead of parenting him or her. Whether you have custody or visitation, you will still have a duty to support your child.

WORKING ON AN AGREEMENT

At some point, you must ultimately consider whether you could both parent your children even with all the negatives, and if so, do you both want to do so? Consider the possibilities.

- What would work best for you, individually, considering your finances, schedule, work or school habits, or needs?

- What is in your best interest?

- If you had sole custody, how would it work with your lifestyle?

- What if the other parent had sole custody?

- How would you fit into that picture?

- What if you both shared custody?

- What would this require?

- How could it work?

Finally, and most importantly, you can begin to focus on what kind of arrangement would be in your child's best interest.

Talk to the Other Parent

Once you have really thought about these issues, talk to the other parent if possible. It may not be an easy thing to do at first, because relationship issues may get in the way. However, if both parents want to continue their relationship with the child, it is important to talk about those relationships whenever possible.

Sometimes it helps to meet in a public place, like a park or a restaurant, to avoid turf issues. Agree to keep the topic of discussion focused on your child. This will help reduce your personal conflicts. Keep in mind that, just like separation is a process, reshaping your relationships with your child is also a process. Recognize that it may take several discussions or meetings before you start shaping a plan for the future care of your child.

Try to begin the first meeting by recognizing that both of you are good parents and both of you need to think about what would be best for your child. Agree that each of you will not simply show up and announce, "I want custody" or "I am entitled to support." Such ultimatums are likely to lead to immediate disagreement and do not leave much room for anything other than bargaining for a position.

Brainstorm the Alternatives

It is easier if you can start by discussing the various alternatives without taking positions. This should be a session of *brainstorming,* where you put all the possibilities down on paper without making any argument for or against any of them. Agree to both consider all of the options on the paper and set a time to meet again to discuss those options.

Some possible options are:

- ✪ sole custody to Mom, child visits Dad;

- ✪ sole custody to Dad, child visits Mom;

- ✪ joint legal custody—child primarily lives with Mom, but sometimes stays with Dad;

- ✪ joint legal custody—child primarily lives with Dad, but sometimes stays with Mom;

- ✪ joint legal and physical custody—child lives part-time with mom and part-time with dad; or,

- ✪ split custody (if more than one child)—Child X lives with Mom and Child Y lives with Dad.

The various matters to consider include:

- ✪ what kind of custody you want;

- ✪ the needs of your child (age, medical, school);

- ✪ your own needs (age, health, work and school schedules);

- ✪ who has the most resources and support (baby-sitters, day care);

- ✪ who will make major decisions and how;

- ✪ who will be responsible for the child's religious training;

- ✪ how much education will you expect the child to receive;

- ✪ the last name of the child;

- ✪ what to do if you or the other parent moves;

- ✪ how to resolve disagreements (mediation); and,

- ✪ what happens if one person violates the agreement.

Use the **Custody and Visitation Checklist** on pages 44 and 45 to help you in formulating your agreement. In the relevant spaces, fill in the information and preferences for each topic.

At the next meeting, assess the options. If some are unacceptable to both of you, delete them. This begins to narrow down the acceptable choices. Now begin to examine the pros and cons of the choices that are left. Make any necessary changes to the choices.

For those choices that are unacceptable to one parent, examine whether there are modifications that would make a choice acceptable to both of you. You need to realize that it is unlikely that you both will be able to agree on all the necessary points at one sitting. Disagreements over issues are common, but they can become the subject of agreement if both parents are willing to compromise and place their child's best interest over all others. Keep in mind that each point you can agree upon is a sign of progress towards your final custody arrangement. Once you both agree to the major points, you can continue to work out the details of remaining points of disagreement. Finally, remember that both of you are the persons with the greatest investment in your child's future.

Tryout Period   If you are able to come to some informal arrangement, try it out for a while to see how it works. Maybe a month or so will allow you to work out the kinks before you look to put your agreement into writing for your court case.

While in this tryout period, log the daily activities that you do with your child. Keep track in the log of how the arrangement worked—what parts of it went well, what parts need to be improved, and how they need to be improved. Document the days and times that need adjustment. If it is feasible, make these adjustments and try it out again for a short period.

Trying it out will hopefully reduce the stress on your child and on yourselves. Agree to meet after the tryout period to make any necessary changes to improve the arrangement.

Your Agreement is Unique

No two families are exactly alike, so no two custody solutions need be exactly the same. While some issues are guided or directed by law, much room for flexibility exists in this area to permit parents to fashion the remainder of their relationship with their minor child in a way that fits their lifestyle. Despite the deterioration of your marriage or relationship, some level of mutual respect for one another as the parent of your child will go far to help a child become a complete adult. That is ultimately what child custody is all about— raising a physically, mentally, and behaviorally well-adjusted child.

MEDIATION

The delay and expense of court cases have led parties in many types of legal cases to try to settle their differences out of court through various types of *alternative dispute resolution* (ADR). Common types of ADR are mediation, conciliation, and arbitration.

In the late 1970s, the rising divorce rates and ongoing problems caused by protracted court battles led courts to look for new solutions to litigation in family cases. Today, ADR may be conducted with parents, grandparents, and third parties.

The most common type of ADR in family law cases is mediation. Another type of ADR, arbitration, where the parties agree to be bound by an arbitrator's ruling, is commonly conducted in various types of civil cases, but not in cases involving child custody, visitation, or support, because courts have an independent duty to determine what is the best interests of a child. Sometimes mediation is included in conciliation court programs.

Mediation is an alternative to a court battle, and is about problem solving; it is not counseling. Because mediation resolves cases earlier, it is less expensive and provides a quicker route to stability, which means less emotional wear on the children. Further, mediation can play a positive role in the willingness of parents to abide by the terms of their custody agreement. As one court has noted, most parents would agree that a stranger is not who they want to determine their child's life.

Mediation results in settlement of custody and visitation issues in more than 70% of cases today. Questions of child support, spousal support, or division of property may or may not be a part of court-sponsored custody mediation programs. For example, some court programs in Florida include child support, spousal maintenance (alimony), and division of property as issues to be mandatorily mediated, as well as parenting issues. Most private mediation will include property, support, and custody or visitation issues.

Mediation is an especially useful tool in nontraditional families, since courts have typically been less willing to recognize the rights of these parties and that it is in the best interests of the child to continue a relationship with a nontraditional parent. For example, in most states, same-sex parents will not need to file for divorce, since they cannot legally marry. Mediation allows a private alternative for these parties.

Defining Mediation

According to model standards adopted in 2005 by the American Bar Association, the American Arbitration Association, and the Association for Conflict Resolution, mediation "is a process in which an impartial third party facilitates communication and negotiation and promotes voluntary decision making by the parties to the dispute."

Mediation allows the parties to a custody case to have flexibility in deciding what is the best interests of their child.

Purposes of Mediation   The adopted standards also explain that there are generally five purposes to mediation. It is a process that provides parties with an opportunity to:

1. define and clarify issues;

2. understand different perspectives;

3. identify interests;

4. explore and assess possible solutions; and,

5. reach mutually satisfactory agreements.

Choosing Mediation   In determining whether voluntary mediation is right for you, consider whether both of you:

✪   can deal fairly with each other;

✪   want to try mediation;

✪   agree to hear what each other has to say; and,

✪   are willing to seek a resolution of your parenting or financial differences.

While mediation can be undertaken before a court case is filed, mediation is a part of all states' family law case processing systems. Mediation may be mandatory or by voluntary request of a party.

Persons Present   Generally, persons other than parties may be included or excluded from being present at mediation sessions by agreement of the parties and the mediator. In some states, the guardian ad litem for the child may be present.

You should not bring your child to mediation, unless notified otherwise by the program. A mediator may choose to interview the child at a future appointment.

Fees Fees for mediation must be disclosed to the parties up front. Today, most private mediators charge hourly fees that may range upwards of $150 per hour. Court-based mediation programs may charge a schedule of fees, a sliding scale fee based on the parties' ability to pay, or an administration fee with the parties paying the mediator directly. In cases where the parties cannot pay a mediator's fee, some courts have mediators available at no cost. Other courts have referrals to private programs that have agreed to charge at a certain fee scale.

While a private mediator can accept unequal fee payments (e.g., one party pays 60%, the other 40%), the fee arrangement is not permitted to play any role in how the mediation is conducted or the outcome of the mediation.

FINDING A MEDIATION PROGRAM

In some states, court mediators work in the courthouse. In others, the courts certify mediators or contract with a bar association or nonprofit corporation to handle court-referred disputes. Mediators may be part of a court-referred program or may be a private agency or individual. Parties who choose voluntary mediation may jointly hire a mediator, who may be an attorney and who should have specific training in mediation techniques. There are national dispute resolution organizations—like The Academy of Family Mediators, The Society of Professionals in Dispute Resolution, and the American Bar Association—that have adopted codes of professional conduct for mediators.

The mediator will facilitate the discussions, but it is the parties who will actually work out their parenting plan and financial support arrangements during the mediation process. Depending upon the complexity of the problems presented and the parties' ability to resolve their parenting or financial differences, the number of mediation sessions will vary.

Mediation sessions may last one to two hours and there may be from one to six sessions, depending on the program. Mediation can even be conducted by telephone conference or email in some cases. Most mediators see the parties together, but may also speak to them individually. Children may be interviewed separately, and sometimes a custody evaluation is requested by the mediator.

Example:

In one program in Los Angeles, the mediator may request a custody evaluation when the mediation has stalled. The evaluator does a thorough investigation of the parties' proposed home environments, and may observe the parties interacting with their child. The evaluator may also interview third parties. At the end of the investigation, the evaluator develops a report for the mediator to help continue the mediation process.

The mediator should provide an overview of the mediation process before you begin. Within the sessions, the mediator will help the parties identify issues, collect information, evaluate options, and find acceptable solutions. Both parties must agree to voluntarily exchange information and documents, and must sign authorizations to obtain information from third parties (employers, insurers, banks, etc.) where necessary. Once the parties have come to an agreement, the mediator will draft a written agreement that can then be signed by both parties and filed with the court clerk.

Sometimes mediators will suggest that, after the agreement is reached, each party have it reviewed by an attorney of their choosing. An attorney may be useful in providing legal advice on the fairness of the proposed agreement, the potential enforcement issues raised, or the likelihood that a court will approve the agreement.

Because mediation is based on each party's concerns being heard and considered, participating in developing the agreement increases the likelihood of cooperation in carrying out the terms of the agreement in the future.

PREPARING FOR MEDIATION

It is important to attend mediation after doing some preparation first. Begin by writing out a list of your concerns and the things you want to accomplish.

One court suggests that a parent prepare by carefully considering two questions.

1. What do you need from the other parent in order to agree to what he or she is asking for?

2. What could you offer that would get the other parent to agree to what you want?

Write a draft of a parenting plan for use when you attend a mediation session. Preparation means you should think about what is in the best interests of the child before you go.

Consider your child's needs and schedules. For example, will you share holidays and birthdays, vacations and travel? How will you work through transportation and exchange of the child? If child support is part of the mediation, consider the issues discussed in Chapter 9.

It is important to be realistic in developing your plan, but be willing to keep and open mind during the mediation. It is just as important to keep focused on the goal of mediation—your child's best interests as you move forward into the future.

What to Bring   Bring relevant documents to the mediation, including the child's school schedule, any report cards, and letters from teachers or therapists. Any police reports that reflect on the child's well-being or on violence in the home should be brought to the mediation. Bring your calendar. If child support will be mediated, bring the relevant financial affidavits you filed with the court.

THE MEDIATOR

The *mediator* is a person who has special training in helping the parties reach their goals. The mediator may or may not be a lawyer or a mental health professional. For example, in California, court mediators have masters' degrees and several years of working with families. Other states list certain number of hours of training required for mediators. Still others require certification by the supreme court of that state.

Most states require court mediators to complete twenty to forty hours of training before they take cases. Some state courts have adopted qualification standards. For example, the Ohio supreme court requires certain qualifications for mediators employed or referred by the court for custody or visitation cases. These family mediators must have:

○ a bachelor's degree or equivalent in education;

○ at least two years of professional experience with families;

○ completion of at least twelve hours of basic mediation training or equivalent experience as a mediator; and,

○ after satisfying the other mentioned requirements, completion of at least forty hours of specialized family or divorce mediation training in a program approved by the Ohio supreme court.

Private mediators should have some training or experience in your type of case, but they need not be attorneys.

Choosing a Mediator

If you are choosing a mediator (or your court referral permits you to choose), consider:

○ whether the mediator provides a free consultation before taking the case;

○ the mediator's fee and scope of services;

○ how mediation will be paid;

○ the number of sessions anticipated;

- the mediator's background (training, education, cases mediated); and,

- most importantly, whether you feel comfortable with the mediator.

Role of the Mediator

Each mediator has his or her own style, but the primary role of the mediator is to help the parties focus on their plausible options with the goal of resolving them. While they do not steer parties toward one option or another, they will focus the parties on various options during the sessions. A mediator usually will make suggestions to the parties, but should not give legal advice. The mediator's expertise can help the parties realistically evaluate the likelihood of certain options.

The mediator should remain impartial, so that the parties can determine what is in the best interests of the child. This means that a mediator must not have any favoritism, bias, or prejudice.

The mediator should not have any prior personal or professional relationship to either party in the case. If there is such a relationship, it must be fully disclosed to the parties. For example, if a mediator had provided mediation services to one party in an earlier case, the mediator should be substituted. If the mediator went to the same church as one of the parties, then the parties should be notified and can decide whether to mediate the case with the mediator. The key is that the mediator must remain impartial for both parties to benefit. If the mediator feels that there is a conflict of interest that could reasonably undermine the goals of mediation, he or she should withdraw from the mediation.

Confidentiality

A mediator must maintain confidentiality of all information obtained during the mediation. However, the mediator can discuss what the parties say with each other. In court-ordered mediation, the mediator can disclose whether the parties appeared for their mediation session and whether they have reached a resolution. Parties can agree to allow the mediator to make additional disclosures.

SETTLING THE CASE

The decision to settle differences in a mediation is up to the parties—not the mediator. This decision should be voluntary and one in which both parties have the necessary information to make the decision to come to an agreement.

WHEN MEDIATION MAY NOT BE APPROPRIATE

If one party is hostile or has real concerns about full and fair disclosure of information, then mediation will not likely assist in settling your differences. Mediation is not usually recommended in cases involving domestic violence or child abuse. Some states do not permit mediation when there is an allegation of domestic violence between the parties. Oregon permits a waiver of mediation when a party files a motion with the court stating that mediation would cause *severe emotional distress*.

Many states permit a domestic violence victim to opt out of mediation or meet separately with the mediator. Even in states that mandate mediation, a party who faces one of these situations can request separate meetings with the mediator and may be able to bring a support person to the mediation.

WHEN THE PARTIES DO NOT AGREE

Parties are not required to reach an agreement in a mediation. In some systems, the mediator will make a recommendation on custody to the court, even where the parties do not agree. Depending on state law, a mediator recommendation may also include tasks for the parties to complete, such as attending anger management classes or parenting classes. Judges often follow this recommendation.

The Contested Custody Case

If the mediation was unsuccessful and the parties cannot otherwise agree, the court must decide the issue for them. Since the judge does not know the parties or the child, this often results in an outcome that is less satisfactory to both parents than if they had compromised to reach an agreement.

BACKGROUND

Because custody is so emotional, a contested custody case is pretty accurately called a *war*. It is all too often an outlet for hostilities between the parents, and the child may be put squarely in the middle and be forced to take sides with one parent or the other.

NOTE: *If you are facing a contested custody case, it is wise to seek consultation with a lawyer before proceeding in court. Because of the emotions involved, it may also be useful to seek mental health assistance before you might actually need it, so that you can be better prepared for the road that lies ahead in a contested custody case. In such a case, you need to realize that your conduct will come under scrutiny for review and consideration. It has been said that during the pendency of a custody case, you will feel like you are living in a fishbowl.*

Educational Programs   In some states, parents are required to attend an educational program in order to learn how their legal battles will affect their child. It is becoming common to require at least a short program to help parents understand the impact of their custody efforts and to help parents assist the child in coping with the emotional fallout from the case. Many courts have guidelines that they provide to parents as part of the process.

The Guardian Ad Litem   As in any litigation where the parties do not agree on what the outcome should be, the custody/visitation proceeding will be considered *adversarial*. The parties are the mother and the father, who (usually) appear with their lawyers. In most states, there will also be another lawyer, called a *guardian ad litem*, who is a person appointed by the court to represent the child's interests.

In order to protect the child's interests independent of the parent's concerns, a growing number of states provide for the appointment of a guardian ad litem. The job of the guardian ad litem is to file any necessary papers with the court on the best interest of the child. The guardian ad litem will interview the child, siblings, and other family members; investigate the school and home situation; and, advise the court as to what would be the best decision for the child. The job of the guardian ad litem is to argue for what he or she believes to be in the child's best interest, which may or may not be what the child wants.

The Judge   The judge's role is to provide a fair forum in which the determination of custody and visitation can be made. As such, the judge's job is not to take sides, but instead to allow each party the opportunity to fully (but also fairly) present his or her case for consideration. However, judges do have their own views and perspective on what is considered commonsense parenting. One big factor in the judge's decision is the credibility of each parent. This is why it is essential to present your case to the judge in the best manner possible. Acts based in anger, frustration, and revenge may affect your credibility as a fit and proper parent.

Child custody and visitation cases are generally considered priority cases by the courts, and judges usually try to move the case along on a fast track as compared to other types of cases.

DISCOVERY

Whether the case is settled by agreement or decided after a trial, both parties require knowledge of all the facts necessary to decide custody, visitation, and child support. Parties can exchange this information voluntarily. If not, there are court rules and procedures in every state that permit a party to obtain this information through a process called *discovery*. A court may enforce discovery by ordering compliance or by punishing the noncompliant party or person.

Interrogatories

A common type of discovery is *interrogatories*. These are written questions that are sent to the other parent and must be answered under oath. The rules concerning interrogatories are governed by your state or local court rules.

Example:

The Los Angeles Superior Court Local Rules state that:

(1) Interrogatories should be used sparingly and never to harass or impose undue burden or expense on adversaries; (2) Interrogatories should not be read by the recipient in an artificial manner designed to assure that answers are not truly responsive; and (3) Objections to interrogatories should be based on a good faith belief in their merit and not be made for the purpose of withholding relevant information. If an interrogatory is objectionable only in part, the unobjectionable portion should be answered.

The court rules will also govern the number and type of questions permitted to be asked. Some states may have standard, approved interrogatories for use in family law cases. Interrogatories usually include sources of income, property, expenses, location of documents or assets, and the names and addresses of potential witnesses. A blank set of family law **INTERROGATORIES** is included in Appendix B. (see form 18, p.246.)

Request to Admit Facts

Another form of discovery is known as a *request to admit facts*, or a *request for admissions*. This is somewhat similar to **INTERROGATORIES**, in that it consists of written statements sent to the other parent that must be responded to under oath. Unlike **INTERROGATORIES**, this form of discovery lists a fact and asks the other parent to admit, deny, or state why the proposed fact cannot be admitted or denied. A request to admit facts may be useful after the answers to the **INTERROGATORIES** have come in and you determine that certain facts are not being disputed. This can save time (and attorney's fees) at trial by focusing on what is in dispute.

Subpoenas Another common form of discovery is a subpoena. A *subpoena* is an order directing the other party or another person to provide certain information, either verbally or by providing documents or other items. For example, a subpoena may be sent to the other parent's employer, bank, or stockbroker in order to obtain financial information. The form of a **SUBPOENA** varies by state, and can often be obtained from the court clerk. (see form 17, p.245.)

Depositions A *deposition* involves asking questions of a party or other person under oath, usually before a court reporter, and having the court reporter make a transcript of the questions and answers. This is a costly form of discovery, because transcripts may run in the hundreds of dollars.

COURT PROCEDURES

The trial of a custody and visitation case is like any other civil case. Each party will have an opportunity to make a brief opening statement. The purpose of an opening statement is to provide an overview of the case.

Your Court Testimony Both parents have an opportunity to testify as to the nature of their relationship with their child and explain why they should have custody. The goal of the case is to determine what is in the best interest of your child. Your testimony to the court should have that goal. Before you testify, you need to have taken the time to think about the *why* of what you are asking the court for. Why is your proposal in the best interest of your child? Why is the other parent's proposal going to have a negative impact on your child? Make sure you have brainstormed all the possibilities before going to court. Attacking the other parent is not generally going to be useful in your testimony. Testimony on negative information should be provided without strong emotions. The court is evaluating who is the person that is most likely to facilitate a cooperative relationship with the other parent, and who truly has the best interest of the child (not themselves) at heart.

Preparation for court will make your testimony much smoother. If possible, familiarize yourself with court procedures. For example, stop in and watch another case being heard. Watch how the judge and the attorneys handle the case.

Your testimony should cover the factors discussed in Chapter 4. If your state's law lists specific factors, you should cover those items. In many states, which parent has been the child's primary caretaker is of special importance.

Example:

Parents will provide testimony on who spends what amount of time with the child and what activities are undertaken during this period. Parents will answer questions like the following.

- Who takes the child to the doctor when he or she is sick?

- Who is the person that gets up in the middle of the night?

- Who changes the baby's diapers?

- Who takes the child back and forth to school activities?

- Who goes to the parent-teacher conferences?

- Who signs the child up for preschool activities?

- Who arranges to have the birthday parties?

Once the testimony establishes the history of the parental relationships with the child, the next issue that must be addressed is how the parents plan to undertake, maintain, or continue their relationship. In this way, the focus turns to the future envisioned by each parent.

In order to measure the parent's future plans, a court will examine how the parties have conducted themselves during the pending case. If a temporary order has been entered, the person with custody must show that he or she has been able to meet the conditions of the custody and visitation arrangement. For instance, has the custodial parent helped to make sure that visitation was provided? The parent with visitation must show how he or she has met the visitation requirements provided in the temporary order. These questions will help the court understand the history of the parents' conduct to better assess whether the parties can place their child's needs and interests above their own in the future.

Cross-Examination

After you have said what you wanted to say, the other parent (or his or her attorney) will have an opportunity to ask you questions about what you have said. The judge may also ask you questions. In answering these questions, you should follow these basic rules.

- ✪ Remain calm.

- ✪ Be straightforward and speak clearly.

- ✪ Listen carefully to the question before answering.

- ✪ If you do not understand a question, say so.

- ✪ Do not volunteer extra information.

- ✪ Try to answer the question as simply as possible.

- ✪ Look at the judge when answering a question.

- ✪ If a question cannot be answered with a yes or no, say so; or explain that you must give two answers to a two-part question.

- ✪ Do not argue with the other parent's attorney or the judge.

Other Witnesses

In addition to your own testimony, you may request other witnesses to appear (either voluntarily or by subpoena) to testify on your behalf. The choice of your other witnesses is determined by the custody, visitation, or child support issues involved. These persons may include friends, family members, neighbors, and your child's teacher, physician, or psychologist.

Keep in mind that before you ask a person to testify on your behalf, you must determine just what that person would say. The last thing you want is a surprise from your own witness. You may be required to provide some basic information for the court about your witnesses, such as their names and what information they have that is relevant to the issue for which they are testifying.

Witnesses (unless they are qualified by the court as expert witnesses) must testify on matters within their own knowledge; so stories, rumors, or gossip (called *hearsay*) are usually not permitted testimony. However, a witness can testify to statements made to the witness by the other parent.

Write out the exact questions you plan to ask each witness. The questions should be short and should address a single point at a time. Allow the witness to answer one question before you pose another one.

Example 1:

Assume you have temporary custody and are seeking sole custody. Your child is in school and you have determined it is important to introduce testimony about your child's school performance, the interactions you have had with the school, and the lack of interactions the other parent has had with the school. You may want your child's teacher to testify. A few questions you might ask the teacher include the following.

- Please state your name.

- What school do you teach at?

- What grade?

- Do you teach {the child}?

- For how long have you taught {the child}?

✪   How is {the child} doing in school?

✪   How is {the child's} attendance at school?

✪   Have you ever participated in parent-teacher conferences with {the other parent} and me?

✪   Has the notice of these conferences been sent to both parents?

✪   Has {the other parent} ever attended these conferences?

✪   To your knowledge, has {the other parent} ever attended any school-related function at which you were present?

If your neighbor has observed significant interactions between you (or the other parent) and your child, you may determine that it is important to show the court the quality of those interactions.

Example 2:
If the other parent failed to show up for the child's last birthday party, and it was devastating to the child, you might ask the witness the following.

✪   Please state your name.

✪   What is your address?

✪   Where is that in relation to my house?

✪   How well do you know {the child and parents}?

✪   What kind of activities have you engaged in with our family over the past number of years?

✪   Did you attend {the child's} birthday party on {date}?

✪   Was {the other parent} present?

✪   What did you see {the child} do as a result?

Expert witnesses. Experts may also testify. Two of the most common types of expert witnesses called to testify in custody cases are psychological and medical experts. Experts may be obtained by the parent or by an order of the court. Their role is to evaluate the parties on the best interest factors. Experts who are appointed by the court will report directly to the court after meeting with the parents and the child, and interviewing them as appropriate. The expert then prepares a report and may also testify as to the report's contents. This evaluation process can take a few months, and may be costly—hundreds or even thousands of dollars.

Admission of Documents

You may wish to put a document into evidence, such as a child's school report card, a medical report, a police report, or the other parent's pay records. A document is usually introduced through the testimony of a witness who can show that the document is authentic and describe the nature of the document. For example, the child's school report card for the previous year may be important proof of how the child is performing in school.

In most courtrooms, the judge will have one or more people to assist with the court's operation. This may include a clerk, a bailiff, and a court reporter. One of these people will have the duty of keeping track of paperwork, including documents and other exhibits offered by the parties. If there are no other court personnel present, then the judge will perform this function. In the example, when the teacher is testifying, you would begin by handing the report card to the appropriate person in the courtroom, and saying "I would like this marked as an exhibit." That person will then mark the exhibit, usually by either placing a sticker on it, stamping it, or writing on it. Usually, one party's exhibits are designated with letters (A, B, C, etc.) and the other party's exhibits are designated with numbers (1, 2, 3, etc.).

After the report card is marked, it will be handed back to you. You will then either hand the report card or a copy of the report card to the other parent or his or her lawyer, so that they understand about what it is you will be asking the teacher. You would next have an exchange with the teacher similar to the following.

Question: Did you prepare any grade reports for my son Jimmy during the past school year?

Answer: Yes.

Question: I am showing you what has been marked as Petitioner's Exhibit A. Do you recognize this document?

Answer: Yes.

Question: What is this document?

Answer: It is my grade report for last year concerning Jimmy.

The other parent (or his or her attorney) has the right to ask the witness questions about the document and to raise any objections to it being used. The most common objections are that the document has not been shown to be authentic and that the document is not relevant to the issues before the court. However, neither of these objections are likely with a teacher and that teacher's grade reports.

When the document is properly shown to have been true and correct, you may ask any relevant questions about your child's grades and refer to the grade report when asking the teacher further questions. Finally, ask the judge to have the grade report admitted into evidence. ("Your honor, I move that Petitioner's Exhibit A be admitted into evidence.") At this point, the other party is entitled to raise any objections he or she might have to the document's being admitted into evidence.

If there were more than one year or semester of grade reports that were relevant, you would go through the same process with each document, having each document assigned its own exhibit number.

The Other Parent's Presentation   After you have finished presenting all of your evidence, the other parent has an opportunity to present his or her evidence. During this phase of the hearing, the roles of you and the other parent are reversed.

That is, he or she has the right to ask questions of the other parent and his or her witnesses (*cross-examination*), and to raise any objections he or she might have to the witnesses' testimony or the documents introduced. However, cross-examination is a skill that not even all lawyers possess, and there are numerous rules of evidence you would need to know to make proper and effective objections. Both cross-examination skills and the rules of evidence are beyond the scope of this book.

Closing Arguments   When each side has completed presenting their evidence, each party has an opportunity to give a *closing argument*. This is where you summarize what you think the evidence shows and state your position as to what you want the judge to do (award you custody, child support, etc.). The judge will then announce his or her decision.

FINAL JUDGMENT

After the judge makes his or her decision, that decision needs to be put in writing in the form of an *order*. Depending upon your state and whether the order is temporary or permanent, this document may be called a *judgment, final judgment, decree, order*, or some similar name. In a case where the parties reach an agreement, instead of repeating all the terms of the agreement in the judgment, the judgment will usually just have a statement that it incorporates the agreement of the parties, thereby giving the agreement binding effect. In a contested case, the judge sets the rules of custody and visitation, which are spelled out in detail in the judgment. The sample **FINAL JUDGMENT** in this book is designed to cover most types of orders a judge might make. (see form 16, p.242.) As with many of the other forms in this book, you may need to modify this form to comply with local requirements and your particular situation.

In either type of case, the judgment binds the parties until it is modified. A modification can take place either as the result of an agreement between the parties (which is approved by the judge), or by one party requesting a change by filing a motion, sometimes called a **PETITION TO MODIFY JUDGMENT OF CUSTODY AND/OR CHILD SUPPORT.** (see form 26, p.262.) After a hearing, if the judge agrees to modify the **FINAL JUDGMENT**, he or she will sign an **ORDER MODIFYING JUDGMENT.** (see form 27, p.266.)

Kidnapping, Abuse, Visitation Problems, and Other Emergencies

Custody battles may take a long time to resolve and may produce emergencies during that period. A parent may take the child and hide him or her to avoid losing the child or because of mistrust with the legal system. A parent who is experiencing domestic violence may need a protective order. A parent may refuse to abide by the temporary custody or visitation orders, necessitating a return to court for enforcement assistance or a change in the order. The court's priority in such emergencies is to protect the child.

If you reasonably suspect criminal behavior on the part of the other parent, report it to authorities in order to get immediate intervention. Today, there are specialized techniques that can help determine whether abuse is present and what needs your child may have as a result of the abuse.

KIDNAPPING

Every year in the United States, thousands of children are taken and hidden by parents or family members. This most often occurs when a parent is afraid of losing custody, or believes the child will be abused or not adequately cared for when with the other parent. While the intent to protect the child may seem noble, kidnapping is still a crime.

Sometimes the parent and the child go into hiding together. Other times, the child is hidden with a parent's relatives or friends, and if the parent is taken into court, he or she either denies knowing where the child is staying or refuses to give such information. In either situation, this certainly creates a serious risk of harm to the child. As a result, kidnapping is considered a form of child abuse. Fathers are reportedly more likely to take their children when there is no child custody order, while mothers are more likely to take their children after a child custody order has been entered.

The risk of kidnapping is higher when one or more of the following situations exist.

- There is considerable animosity between the parents.

- A parent threatens to kidnap the child.

- A parent lives, works, or is preparing to move out of state.

- There are allegations of physical or sexual abuse, and a parent feels the courts are slow in reaction and fears for the child's life or welfare.

Preventing Kidnapping

If you believe that a risk of kidnapping exists, you may try to minimize the chances by one or more of the following actions.

- Ask your local police or prosecutor to warn the other parent that kidnapping is a crime.

- If you already have a custody order, give a *certified* copy of that order to your school, day care center, and baby-sitter. (You can obtain a certified copy from the court clerk.) Tell them not to release your child to anyone except on your direction.

- If the child is old enough, teach him or her how to contact you, including your telephone number and instructions on how to use the telephone to call home.

- ✪ Keep identifying information about the other parent and the child, such as a current photograph, Social Security information, driver's license number, and financial account numbers.

- ✪ If the other parent lives out of state, file a certified copy of your custody order in that state to let the courts know of its existence. A certified copy can be obtained from the clerk of the court that issued the custody order. By filing a certified copy of your custody order with the clerk of the out-of-state parent's local court, both your state and the other parent's state will recognize and enforce the custody order pursuant to the Uniform Child Custody Jurisdiction Act or the Uniform Child Custody Jurisdiction Enforcement Act. The court clerks maintain a registry of orders to facilitate communication and enforcement. You may file by mail. There may be a filing fee to register your custody order.

Preventive Court Orders

Court orders may also assist in preventing kidnapping by restricting visitation conditions, supervising visitation, or by prohibiting a parent from taking the child on a trip outside the state without prior court approval. If the fear is that the parent with custody will take the child, the same restrictions can be placed on that parent.

Parents may also be required to post money with the court in the form of a bond (usually an insurance policy) as security for the return of a child. If the parent does kidnap the child, the proceeds can help pay for the search to find and return the child.

If Your Child is Kidnapped

Criminal penalties exist for kidnapping. If your child is kidnapped, you should call the police and report your child as missing.

If you have not yet obtained a custody order, you should file for custody. If you do have a custody order, the *Uniform Child Custody Jurisdiction Act* (UCCJA) or the *Uniform Child Custody Jurisdiction Enforcement Act* (UCCJEA) are designed to prevent the other parent from taking the child and crossing state lines to file for a new custody order. All fifty states have adopted the UCCJA, with nearly all adopting its successor, the UCCJEA. Courts will recognize and enforce orders made in other states. In other words, your order will be recognized as binding even if the other parent tries to get a later order. Contempt penalties may also be entered in your court proceeding against the other parent.

You should also look for your child. The *Parental Kidnapping Prevention Act* (PKPA) is a federal law that permits the federal government to assist in locating parents who have taken their child in violation of a court order. This is done through the *Federal Parent Locator Service*, which will search computer files on address information for the kidnapping parent.

When your child is found, make sure you file your custody order with the clerk's office where the child is located and request that police help you in picking up your child.

DOMESTIC VIOLENCE AND CHILD ABUSE

Sadly, the number of parents who are accused during a custody battle of abusing their children has increased over the years. The issue usually arises in connection with an allegation of sexual abuse. Once this type of charge is made, the parties are not likely to settle the custody case, and the cost of litigation is high.

These cases are often lengthy, and sometimes are resolved only after thorough psychological and home studies are completed on the parents and child to determine the truth and accuracy of the allegations. If the child has been abused, he or she will need the appropriate protection, enforceable through court orders. If the child has not been abused, it is important to resume his or her relationship with both parents as soon as possible.

Even if the case is decided by a trial, the matter is not always over. If one party believes that the court decided wrongly in giving the other party custody or visitation, that parent may flee with the children or may send the child away to live with others for protection. The parents may continue the court battle, perhaps resulting in the parent who refuses to produce the child being held in contempt or even prosecuted for child abduction.

Protective Orders

Every state provides for *protective orders* prohibiting domestic abuse. These orders are usually filed with the local police and may permit police to arrest a parent upon a violation. Although these orders may be pursued by an attorney, many court clerk's offices have protective order packets available. These are written in simple, clear language and can be filed and heard in court, usually within a very short period of time. These orders may be permanent, but they commonly last for some specified duration of time (e.g., two years) to protect the abused person (and the child) from specified types of behavior that may include stalking, following, threatening, harassing, and physical violence.

Privacy of name and address. Many states recognize that the victim of abuse is put at greater risk when having to disclose a new name or address. Therefore, petitions for protective orders, as well as petitions for divorce, custody, and support, may be filed without having to disclose this information. Check with your jurisdiction before putting this information in your petition.

VISITATION PROBLEMS

One common source of problems for parents in cases of sole custody is a parent's right to visitation. This is especially true in the many cases where the court order simply says the noncustodial parent is entitled to *reasonable* or *reasonable and liberal visitation*. When parents do not get along, the questions then become, "What is the definition of reasonable?" and "Who decides what is reasonable?"

To help avoid disputes, the order should be as specific as possible about visitation rights. The order should set forth the starting and ending days and times for visitation, and allocate vacations, holidays, birthdays, and other special days or events. If telephone access is contemplated, this should also be addressed in the order. (See earlier chapters and the **PARENTING PLAN** forms in Appendices A and B for suggested language.)

Sometimes, a parent's abuse of visitation will be sufficient to change the visitation or even the custody order. For example, in a case where the custodial parent continually interferes with the visitation rights of the other parent, the parent who is denied reasonable visitation rights can go back to court and seek a change in the order to be more specific about when visitation will occur. Occasionally, where the custodial parent demonstrates a refusal to comply with any visitation order, judges have changed custody to the parent who has been denied visitation.

Some situations require *supervised* or *monitored* visitation orders. These cases might involve situations where a parent presents a danger to the child, where the child has been kidnapped previously, or where threats have been made to kidnap the child.

Supervised Visitation

The person given the responsibility for supervising the visits may be a law enforcement officer, social worker, clergyperson, relative, family friend, or any person (or agency) designated by the court or agreed upon by the parties.

While not yet available everywhere, *visitation centers* have been a growing phenomenon over the past decade. These centers provide a neutral, supervised location within which visitation may be monitored. The staff have training in custody issues and will protect the child if needed. In cases where there has been an incident of abuse or parental neglect, the family may be ordered to have visitation at one of these centers.

Exchange of the Child

Exchanging a child for visitation often requires some level of contact between the parents. When there is a high degree of anger or frustration between the parents, this contact can lead to a refusal to produce or return the child in a timely fashion. It may also lead to arguing in the presence of the child over other issues (often child support).

Some parents decide to make the exchange in a public place where there are witnesses. In other cases, visitation may begin and end at a neutral location, such as a visitation agency, in which the parent with custody drops the child and the visiting parents takes and returns the child. In this way, parents can reduce their contacts with one another. The details of how the exchange will take place can also be included in the order or parenting plan.

Mediation and Court Orders

If there is a problem with visitation, and the parties agree, the issue could be the subject of mediation in an effort to work out the differences to a mutually agreeable solution. Without an agreement to mediate, the court may order mediation. However, if the parents cannot agree that they want to try mediation, it is unlikely that court-ordered mediation would be successful.

Child Support

The laws of all states provide that every parent has a legal duty to support his or her child. This is true whether the parents are married or not, and whether the child lives with them or not. In addition, any person who has custody of a child may be eligible to seek an order for child support. This includes nontraditional custodians, such as grandparents, stepparents, extended family members, same-sex parents, or other third parties.

HISTORY OF CHILD SUPPORT

Historically, judges examined each parent's ability to pay and the needs of the child in determining child support. Even so, many parents were not awarded child support. As late as the mid-1980s, over 30% of the more than eight million parents who had custody of their children were not awarded any child support at all.

Worse still, parents who were supposed to pay child support were not paying as required by their orders.

Example:
One study showed that in 1989, of the half-million women due child support, 24% received partial payment and 25% received nothing.

The problems with child support awards came to the attention of the federal government because public subsidies increasingly took over when parents did not pay. To make child support more fair and certain, the federal government now requires every state to adopt guidelines for use in determining child support.

Federal Action   In the *Personal Responsibility and Work Opportunity Reconciliation Act of 1996*, the federal government mandated sweeping changes to child support laws. States are now required to pass uniform interstate laws that provide for uniform rules, procedures, and forms for interstate child support cases.

In 1998, all states were required to adopt the *Uniform Interstate Family Support Act* (UIFSA). These provisions are designed to help track parents who move across state lines.

The federal law also requires states to establish *central registries* of child support orders, centralized collection and disbursement units, and expedited procedures for child support enforcement. Further, states must have registries of newly hired employees, have laws and procedures to make it easier to establish paternity, and strengthen penalties for failure to pay child support.

As a result of these federal initiatives, the government has cracked down on parents who do not pay support.

THE BASICS

The legal obligation to support a child includes the child's basic living needs—such as housing, food, and clothing expenses—as well as medical costs and other expenses such as education, after-school activities, and vacation expenses.

It must be noted that child support is not always limited to the payment of money. For example, part of a child support order in a divorce case may award the family home to the parent with custody until the child reaches the age of majority, with the noncustodial parent paying some or all of the mortgage, insurance, and property tax payments during that time. On the other hand, once a dollar amount for child support has been ordered by a court, it must be paid in money. Gifts of clothing and other items in lieu of money will not be credited against the support amount due, unless a court gives the parent prior permission to do so.

Who Gets Support

Any parent (or person who has legal custody of a child) may be eligible to seek an order for child support from a parent.

How You Get Support

Child support is typically raised as an issue in divorce proceedings, custody actions, and paternity (also called *parentage*) cases. In divorce cases, some states combine child support with support for a spouse into a *family support order*. A person seeking child support may also file an independent case to establish a child support order.

The parent (or other eligible person) may also file an application for child support enforcement services with a state agency. Every state has a child support enforcement program that is usually operated by the state's social services agency, the state attorney general's office, or some other agency. Persons who are receiving governmental financial assistance, such as *Medicaid* or *Aid to Families with Dependent Children* (AFDC) are eligible to receive state support enforcement services for free. Some states charge a small fee for persons who are not receiving state aid.

Who Pays

Both parents share responsibility to support their child whether they are married to each other or not. This is true even if the parent is a minor.

Example:

In one Illinois case, a father, who was 15 years old at the time his child was born to his girlfriend, argued that because he was a child himself, he did not have an adult's duty of child support. The court rejected this argument, finding that the child's right to support outweighed the father's rights as a minor. (*In re Parentage of J.S.*, 550 N.E.2d 257 (Ill.App. 1990).)

If the parents have married, the support obligation exists before, during, and after the marriage. It is a joint obligation. In some cases, even the parent who has full custody may be ordered to pay child support to the other parent while the child visits, because the decision of custody does not automatically answer the question of who should pay support.

HOW SUPPORT IS DETERMINED

Child support is determined by examining both parents' ability to pay and measuring the child's support requirements. Because every state examines and weighs factors somewhat differently, the two most common methods for how support is determined are shown in this chapter. (On pages 103–104, you will learn about various states' guidelines.)

When parents come to an agreement on child support, they often agree on a support amount above the basic guidelines of their state law. This is because the guidelines are minimum threshold amounts. Parents who have the ability often agree that providing their child with a comfortable standard of living requires a support amount above the guideline amounts.

FACTORS IN SETTING CHILD SUPPORT

The amount of support is based on a number of factors, with the goal being to make reasonable provisions for the welfare of the child. Factors to be considered include:

✪   the financial resources of the child and parents;

✪   the physical and emotional condition of the child; and,

✪   the child's educational needs.

State guidelines also factor these items into their payment schedules. If the parents were married, misconduct during the marriage (such as adultery) will generally *not* be considered in determining child support.

Financial Resources

To be enforceable, any child support order must take into account the ability of the parents to pay the amount needed. Financial resources means more than just income. Also considered will be the parent's assets (such as bank accounts and property) and standards of living.

Needs of the Child

Perhaps the most overriding factor for determining child support is the needs of the child. State guidelines identify a basic level of need. While "needs" means more than just basic living requirements, it does not include unnecessary expenses, such as summer camps or leisure activities. If the parents have been married, a court may look at the standard of living the child had prior to the divorce or separation of the parents. If so, the determination of child support will attempt to maintain that standard of living for the child.

Health Insurance

Health care is a required element of state guidelines. If the parents do not agree to provide health insurance, the court will order it paid regardless of which parent has custody.

Example:
In any child support case in Louisiana, the court may order one of the parties to enroll or maintain an insurable child in a health benefits plan, policy, or program. In determining which parent should be required to enroll the child or to maintain such insurance on behalf of the child, the court considers each parent's individual, group, or employee health insurance program; employment history; and personal income and other resources. The cost of health insurance premiums incurred on behalf of the child are added to the basic child support amount.

Other states provide for a health insurance coverage assignment. This means that a court order is entered that requires the noncustodial parent's employer (or other person providing health insurance to the noncustodial parent) to enroll the child in the parent's health insurance plan. The order also authorizes the employer of the noncustodial parent to deduct the cost of the health care premiums from the noncustodial parent's earnings.

States also provide for the award of extraordinary medical expenses where appropriate. In Kentucky, for example, this would include medical, surgical, dental, orthodontal, optometric, nursing, and hospital services.

Educational Expectations

The reasonable education expenses of a child may be agreed to, or the court may order a parent (or both) to pay for the education of a child. Some courts limit these expenses to public school education, but where the party has the ability to pay, a court may order payment for the cost of a private school and even a boarding school.

Most parents agree to pay college expenses. Although a college education may not be considered a necessity by some courts, where the parent has the ability to pay, the court may order the parent to support a child after high school, through technical school or college. For example, Connecticut courts can compel parents to pay the equivalent of a four-year state college expense until the child turns 23 years old if it is more likely than not that the parents would have provided such support without a divorce. Not all states permit this. A law in New Hampshire prohibits a court order for educational expenses beyond high school in the absence of the parties' agreement. If educational expenses are ordered, courts consider the parent's ability to pay and the child's capacity and ability.

Other Expenses

Parents may also agree, or the court may order a parent, to pay for various other expenses for a child, such as summer camps and vacation costs. One common item in the "other" category is child care costs while a parent is completing an education or job hunting. Many state guidelines address this as an adjustment to the support obligation. In addition, all states' guidelines address extraordinary expenses and allow courts to make adjustments based on the best interests of the child.

Guidelines   All states have guidelines that help to determine the basic amount of support for a child. There is no single guideline model used in every state, but the states generally set forth their basic principles in their guidelines. It is important to note that the guidelines in each state are required to be reviewed at least every four years, so they may change. If you are researching your state's guidelines, make sure you are using the most recent version of them. (See **www.sphinxlegal.com/extras/rightstochildcustody** for your state's law citations and the section on "Legal Research" in Chapter 1 for how to find the law in your state.)

Parents may agree to child support that is outside the guidelines. Although adjustments can be, and often are, made to the guideline amounts, generally a court (or administrative agency if permitted) must make a written finding that the application of the guidelines would be unjust or inappropriate in a particular case.

Each state lists the main principles of their guidelines. The following California statute explains in detailed fashion the objectives of the state's guidelines.

In implementing the statewide uniform guideline, courts shall adhere to the following principles.

(a) A parent's first and principal obligation is to support his or her minor children according to the parent's circumstances and station in life.

(b) Both parents are mutually responsible for the support of their children.

(c) The guideline takes into account each parent's actual income and level of responsibility for the children.

(d) Each parent should pay for the support of the children according to his or her ability.

(e) The guideline seeks to place the interests of children as the state's top priority.

(f) Children should share in the standard of living of both parents. Child support may therefore appropriately improve the standard of living of the custodial household to improve the lives of the children.

(g) *Child support orders, in cases in which both parents have high levels of responsibility for the children, should reflect the increased costs of raising the children in two homes and should minimize significant disparities in the children's living standards in the two homes.*

(h) *The financial needs of the children should be met through private financial resources as much as possible.*

(i) *It is presumed that a parent having primary physical responsibility for the children contributes a significant portion of available resources for the support of the children.*

(j) *The guideline seeks to encourage fair and efficient settlements of conflicts between parents and seeks to minimize the need for litigation.*

(k) *The guideline is intended to be presumptively correct in all cases, and only under special circumstances should child support orders fall below the child support mandated by the guideline formula.*

(l) *Child support orders must ensure that children actually receive fair, timely, and sufficient support reflecting the state's high standard of living and high costs of raising children compared to other states.*

Similarly, the Idaho guidelines state the same general principles, but word them a bit differently.

(a) *Both parents share legal responsibility for supporting their child. That legal responsibility should be divided in portion to their guidelines income, whether they be separated, divorced, remarried, or never married.*

(b) *In any proceeding where child support is under consideration, child support shall be given priority over the needs of the parents or creditors in allocating family resources. Only after careful scrutiny should the court delay implementation of the guidelines amount because of debt assumption.*

(c) *Support shall be determined without regard to the gender of the custodial parent.*

(d) *Rarely should the child support obligation be set at zero. If the monthly income of the paying parent is below $800 the Court should carefully review the incomes and living expenses to determine the maximum amount of support that* *can reasonably be ordered without denying a parent the means for self-support at a minimum subsistence level. There shall be a rebuttable presumption that a minimum amount of support is at least $50 per month per child.*

All of the states' guidelines assist in identifying minimum amounts to be paid for child support, and offer schedules of income and allowable expenses to calculate the presumed award amount. Even though the guidelines exist, each case is examined on its own merits, because no two families have exactly the same obligations and needs. The guidelines recognize this, and there are provisions for adjustments to the guideline amounts.

Defining Income   Income used to determine child support may be gross income or net income, depending on your state's guidelines. *Gross income* will be defined by the guidelines, and will usually include money, property, or services from most sources, whether or not it is reported or taxed under federal law. If *net income* is used, the law will usually define what is included in gross income and what deductions are allowed in computing the net income. Under either method, income from public assistance programs is usually exempted.

Example:

Idaho's guidelines, which use the parents' gross incomes, define gross income as income from any source and includes, but is not limited to:

income from salaries, wages, commissions, bonuses, dividends, pensions, interest, trust income, annuities, social security benefits, workers' compensation benefits, unemployment insurance benefits, disability insurance benefits, alimony, maintenance, any veteran's benefits received, education grants, scholarships, other financial aid, and disability and retirement payments to or on behalf of a child.

Idaho courts may consider when and for what duration the receipt of funds from gifts, prizes, net proceeds from property sales, severance pay, and judgments will be considered as available for child support. Unlike some states, benefits received by a parent from public assistance programs in Idaho are included as income (except in cases of extraordinary hardship).

Recognizing that parents sometimes try to quit their jobs to avoid paying support, a court may use the parent's *earning capacity* rather than actual earnings to determine support. Earning capacity is based on the parent's education, training, and work experience, and the availability of work in or near the parent's community.

Example:

A noncustodial parent voluntarily quits a job paying $40,000 a year and works part-time for $12,000. The court may use the earning capacity of $40,000—not the actual gross income of $12,000—to determine the amount of child support.

Some state guidelines set out certain deductions from gross income to arrive at a net income figure from which the child support is determined. These deductions vary between states by type and amount, but standard deductions generally include:

- ✪ taxes;

- ✪ Social Security deductions;

- ✪ health insurance;

- ✪ mandatory retirement contributions; and,

- ✪ prior child support.

States may also permit subtractions from gross income for certain identified reasonable expenses. For example, in Wisconsin, gross income could be reduced by business expenses that the court determines are reasonably necessary for producing that income or operating the business.

Combined Income Guidelines

Many state's guidelines determine child support by combining the income of the parents, then calculating the guideline percentage of income available for support from each parent. This model is often called the *income shares model*. For example, the Indiana Child Support Guidelines use this model and explain that it is based "on the concept that the child should receive the same proportion of parental income that he or she would have received if the parents lived together."

Determining child support under this model generally involves five basic steps (although it may take several state worksheet pages to cover these steps).

1. Identify the gross and net income of each parent.

2. Add the income of each parent together for a combined total income.

3. Find the child support due for that total income amount on your state's guideline.

4. Add or deduct the amounts that are permitted by your state.

5. Determine the proportionate share due from each parent.

States that use this model recognize that the parent who has caretaking responsibilities will pay the support directly for the child, while the other parent will pay a dollar figure for child support.

For example, calculate child support for one child in Alabama.

1. Assume that the parent with custody has a gross income of $1,000 per month, while the noncustodial parent has a gross income of $2,000 per month.

2. The incomes are added: $3,000.

3. Next, look to the Alabama child support schedule chart to determine the guideline amount:

Combined Gross Income	1 *	2 *	3 *	4 *	5 *	6 *
2900	426	660	826	931	1015	1085
2950	431	669	837	944	1029	1100
3000	437	677	848	956	1042	1114
3050	443	686	859	969	1056	1129
* Refers to number of children						

The guideline calls for a total child support sum of $437.

4. Prorate the basic child support sum ($437) between the parents, based on their income: the noncustodial parent will pay two-thirds of the total due, or $291. For this example, we are assuming no special adjustments are needed. (*Prorate* means to determine the appropriate share owed by a party, as in "the child support was prorated between the parents based on the percentage of their income to the total amount of support due.")

A similar result would be reached in Virginia.

1. Once again, the parents incomes would be added for a combined income of $3,000.

2. Look at the guidelines in the Virginia law to determine the child support due, which would be $445.

Combined Gross Income	1 *	2 *	3 *	4 *	5 *	6 *
2850	430	667	836	941	1027	1098
2900	435	675	846	953	1039	1112
2950	440	683	856	964	1052	1125
3000	445	691	866	975	1064	1138
3050	443	686	859	969	1056	1129
* Refers to number of children						

3. Add any allowable adjustments. For this example, assume there is a $50 expense for child care and a $15 expense for extraordinary medical expenses. That would bring the total to $510.

4. Under Virginia's scheme, you would prorate the amount due between the custodial parent and noncustodial parent. The noncustodial parent would pay child support under the Virginia guidelines of $340. (This is two-thirds of $510.)

Percentage Income Guidelines

Another type of guideline commonly used is based on the percentage of income of the noncustodial parent. Some states use a flat percentage, while in other states the percentage depends on the level of income of the parent. Although the method of determining the child support is different, the result, if the previous example is used, is not too much different from the states above.

Determining child support under this model generally involves three steps.

1. Identify the gross and net income of the parent who does not have custody.

2. On your state's guideline, find the percentage of income due for child support.

3. Add or deduct the amounts that are permitted by your state.

The percentage of income guidelines in Wisconsin are typical. Wisconsin law establishes that child support amounts are based on the belief that both parents are responsible for supporting their children, and both parents will support their child whether they live together or apart. Although this type of guideline looks only at the income of the parent without custody, it again assumes that the parent who has caretaking responsibilities will pay his or her share of the support directly for the child, while the other parent will pay a dollar figure for child support. The Wisconsin guidelines are as follows:

	17% of gross income
one child	17% of gross income
two children	25% of gross income
three children	29% of gross income
four children	31% of gross income

As reflected in the following chart illustration, if a noncustodial parent's gross monthly income was $1,200, and there was one child, the support would be $204 (17% of gross income). If there were two children, the amount would increase to $300, or 25% of the gross income.

Noncustodial Parent's Gross Income	1 *	2 *	3 *	4 *
	17%	25%	29%	31%
1,200	204	300	348	372
2,000	340	500	580	620
* Refers to number of children				

To compare the guideline amounts with those in our combined income guideline states, look at the earlier example of the noncustodial parent's income of $2,000. In Wisconsin, the chart above shows that the guideline percentage for one child is 17%. Seventeen percent of $2,000 is $340. Notice how this is very close to both examples previously mentioned (Alabama and Virginia) using the combined income guidelines. The point is that, while states have different methods of reaching the basic support levels, they often lead to similar support amounts.

Adjustments   Many states permit add-on amounts or special adjustments. These may increase or decrease the basic support obligation. While each state has its own adjustment definitions, most include:

- ✪ extraordinary medical, psychological, dental, or educational expenses;

- ✪ independent income or assets of child;

- ✪ child support, alimony, or spousal maintenance previously ordered;

- ✪ age or special needs of child;

- ✪ split or shared custody arrangements; and,

- ✪ which parent takes the IRS dependency exemption.

States may also add other bases for adjusting child support orders.

Example:

In addition to the previously mentioned factors, the Florida guidelines state that a court may adjust child support based upon such things as:

- ✪ the payment of support for a parent that regularly has been paid and for which there is a demonstrated need;

- ✪ seasonal variations in one or both parents' incomes or expenses;

- ✪ the greater needs of older children;

- ✪ special needs (such as costs that may be associated with the disability of a child) that have traditionally been met within the family budget even though the fulfilling of those needs will cause the support to exceed the proposed guidelines;

- ✪ when application of the child support guidelines requires a person to pay another person more than 55% percent of his or her gross income for a child support obligation for current support resulting from a single support order;

- ✪ any other adjustment that is needed to achieve an equitable result, such as a reasonable and necessary existing expense or debt; or,

- ✪ the particular shared parental arrangement, such as where the children spend a substantial amount of their time with the secondary residential parent (reducing the financial expenditures incurred by the primary residential parent), the refusal of the secondary residential parent to become involved in the activities of the child, or giving due consideration to the primary residential parent's home-making services. (If a child has visitation with a noncustodial parent for what the court determines is a significant amount of time, the court may reduce the amount of support paid by the noncustodial parent during the time of visitation.)

Courts must state the reasons for a departure from the guideline amounts.

Example:
In California, if the support order differs from the guidelines, a court must explain, in writing or on the record:

✪ the amount of support that would have been ordered under the guideline formula;

✪ the reasons the amount of support ordered differs from the guideline formula amount; and,

✪ the reasons the amount of support ordered is consistent with the best interests of the children.

Preexisting Child Support Order

One of the most common scenarios that affect the support guidelines is where a parent has been divorced before and has a previous court order to pay child support. Even though there is a second family, it does not mean that the paying parent's responsibility to the first family ends. However, the amount of support in the second case can be affected because that parent has the responsibility for supporting his or her other children. In these situations, the guidelines may factor in, as a deduction from income, the amount of the first child support order.

Example:

A man was divorced from his first wife in 2000, and is subject to a court order to pay monthly child support of $350 for a child from that marriage. He is now going through a divorce from his second wife, with whom he has a child. His guideline income is $3,000 per month. The guidelines would subtract the first child support ordered amount from his income ($3,000 - $350 = $2,650), then determine the support for the second child by applying the guidelines to the new income figure of $2,650.

Shared or Joint Custody

State guidelines deal with joint or shared custody arrangements in a number of ways. In some cases where the parents share nearly equal parenting time, each parent's pro rata share of support offsets the other's, so that they do not exchange support. Instead, each parent essentially pays all costs when the child is with him or her. In other cases, custody may be shared, but one parent spends more physical time with the child. In such cases, prorating the total amount due for child support and factoring in the parenting time will once again yield a sum to be paid for support.

Some states include tables in their guidelines for adjusting the guideline amounts based on the percentage of shared parenting time.

Example:

If both parents were required to spend 17% percent of their income on their child and Parent A had an income of $2,000 per month and Parent B had an income of $1,500 per month, their initial child support due would be:

Parent A $2,000 x 17% = $340

Parent B $1,500 x 17% = $255

However, if Parent A spends 44% (or 160 days) of the time with the child and Parent B spends the remaining 56% (or 205 days), the state guideline schedule below prorates the amount of child support due.

Percent of time with child	Percent of original child support amount
43	56.71
44	53.38
45	50.05
46	46.72
47	43.39
48	40.06
49	36.73
50	33.40
51	30.07
52	26.74
53	23.41
54	20.08
55	16.75
56	13.42

Now, apply the percentages from the table:

Parent A owes 53.38% of the original total ($340 x .5338 = $181.49)

Parent B owes 13.42% of the original total ($255 x .1342 = $34.22)

Final calculations would show that $147.27 ($181.49 - $34.22) was due Parent B from Parent A. This works out to a percentage due of 7.36%.

The previous is just one example of how state guidelines approach the shared parenting arrangement. Your state may treat this issue differently in its guidelines. Your local worksheets will help you calculate the proper amounts.

Split Custody   States also attempt to apply their guidelines to cases in which the parents have more than one child and have sole custody of some, but not all, of their children.

Example:

If Parent A in such a case has custody of one of the three children under state percentage of income guidelines, then Parent A might pay 25% of his or her income as child support (for the other two children). Parent B would owe the guideline 17% for the one child in Parent A's custody.

If their incomes are $3,000 for Parent A and $1,500 for Parent B, support would be calculated as follows.

Parent A: $3,000 x 25% = $750 (2 children)

Parent B: $1,500 x 17% = $255 (1 child)

Parent A owes Parent B the sum of $495 ($750 - $255 = $495) in child support.

Visitation arrangements may result in an adjustment to a child support order.

Example:

Some states prorate support based on time spent with each parent. In Nebraska, the guidelines permit a reduction of 50% for visitation periods of four weeks or more. In addition, a court may adjust support due if visitation requires long-distance transportation costs.

Tax Consequences   Under current federal tax law, child support payments are neither deductible for the paying parent nor taxable to the receiving parent.

Ordinarily, the tax law presumes that the parent with custody is entitled to take the tax exemption for their child. (See the section on "Taxes and Custody" in Chapter 2.) If the paying parent who does not have custody desires to take the deduction, the parent with custody must sign IRS Form 8332, or a similar statement agreeing not to claim the child's exemption. That agreement may cover one year, a number of years (for example, alternate years), or for all future years.

NOTE: *In some states, the actual federal and state income tax benefits of the parent who claims the federal child dependency exemption will be considered in making a child support award.*

Because the revenue rules do change periodically, check with your local IRS office for the proper form and filing requirements.

Filing for bankruptcy will not relieve a party from paying child support, because child support is not dischargeable in bankruptcy. (See United States Code, Chapter 11, Section 523(a)(5).)

Child Support Agreements

Like custody decisions, cooperative decisions concerning child support can work to the benefit of all parties, especially your child. A court will consider the terms of an agreement concerning support. Where it is just and reasonable under your state's laws and the circumstances, the judge will award the agreed-upon amount. The amount and terms of your support agreement will then be included in your custody or visitation judgment.

If the judge determines, however, that the amount agreed upon is not fair or reasonable based on the laws of your state or the circumstances, your agreement will not be binding on the court. The judge may then choose to make an award of child support that is different from that upon which you have agreed. The primary consideration will be whether your agreement is in the child's best interests.

Example:
An agreement that in essence says "If you don't ask for visitation, I won't ask for child support" is unacceptable to the courts in all states and will not be approved. No court would consider such an arrangement to be in a child's best interest,

and parties will not be permitted to use their agreement to prevent a court from making a reasonable child support order.

This holds true for any other order that serves the best interests of the child.

FACTORS TO CONSIDER

In agreeing on a child support amount, the parties should consider a number of factors, including:

- ✪ what the state's guideline requires;

- ✪ additional quality of life or standard of living issues;

- ✪ each parent's financial resources;

- ✪ the needs of the child;

- ✪ who will be responsible for health care expenses;

- ✪ what educational expenses will be paid;

- ✪ other expenses;

- ✪ who takes the tax exemption;

- ✪ when and how payments will be made;

- ✪ whether there will be security (such as a trust or life insurance) for the payments;

- ✪ what happens if the paying parent dies; and,

- ✪ if there is more than one child, what effect it has on the payments if a child dies, reaches the age of majority (18 or 21), marries, or joins the military.

THE APPROPRIATE GUIDELINE

In the previous chapter, you generally learned about the child support guidelines in effect in every state. The guidelines that cover your case will be found either in your state's statutes, administrative rules, or court opinions. You can obtain the exact guidelines from your legal resource library. Many states also list their guidelines on the Internet, but be aware that these are not necessarily the most current version. You can also contact your local child support enforcement agency for information on obtaining your state's guidelines.

Working through your state's guidelines may feel a bit like doing your taxes. Many states provide specific worksheets and forms to assist in the process. These are available through your local clerk's offices or your local child support enforcement agency. With your state's guidelines as a basis, you can formulate an amount of child support to put into your agreement on custody and visitation.

YOUR BASIC GUIDELINE AMOUNT

The guidelines of all the states are based upon the income of one or both of the parents. Some states use the *combined income* of the parents, while other states just look at the income of the parent who will be paying support (often referred to as the *payor* or the *obligor*). States also differ in how they determine what income is used to calculate support. Therefore, in calculating the amount of support to expect in your case, you will first need to determine two things.

1. Does your state use the combined income method or the percentage of the payor's income method?

2. Does your state use gross income or net income?

To help you calculate child support, you will find a **COMBINED INCOME CHILD SUPPORT WORKSHEET** on page 128 and a **PERCENTAGE OF INCOME CHILD SUPPORT WORKSHEET** on page 129. To determine which of these worksheets to use, you will need to read your state's guidelines to find out which method is used. If combined income is used, you will begin by determining the amount of monthly income that both parents have. If your state uses a percentage of the paying parent's income, you will begin by determining the income of the parent without custody.

NOTE: *You will need to read your state's guidelines to determine whether gross income or net income is used. If your state uses the gross income method, the income from the sources listed will be the basis for calculating the support amount.*

Gross Income   Your state's guidelines will probably begin with a definition of *income* or *gross income*. This will basically be income from various sources, without any deduction for taxes, Social Security, etc.

Example:
Your state might include the following in its definition:

- salary, wages, interest, and dividends;

- commissions, allowances, overtime, and tips;

- business income;

- disability benefits;

- workers' or unemployment compensation;

- pension or retirement payments;

- Social Security benefits; and,

- maintenance, alimony, or spousal support.

Net Income   If your state uses *net income*, you will need to deduct from gross income the permitted deductions that are set forth in the guidelines. Typically, this includes:

- federal, state, and local income taxes;

- FICA, Medicare, or self-employment taxes;

- mandatory union dues and retirement payments;

○ health insurance (but not for the child, as this will be considered separately later in the calculation);

○ maintenance, alimony, or spousal support paid; and,

○ child support for other children.

Combined Income

In combined income states, you next add the final income amounts for each parent to get his or her combined income. In a percentage state, you only calculate the guideline amount from the paying parent (so do not combine incomes in those states).

Adjustments to Income

Regardless of whether your state uses gross or net income, check your state's guidelines to determine if there are any unusual expenses that can be deducted.

Apply Guidelines

Once you have the income calculated, look to your state's guidelines to determine the amount of support to be paid at that income level. On the guideline schedule for your state (usually this is a chart of some kind), you will find the amount due for the income amount and the number of children for whom support is to be paid.

Combined income method. In combined income states, the chart will usually give you what is considered the minimum monthly amount required to raise that number of children. You then determine the proportionate share due from each parent.

Percentage of income method. In percentage of income states, the chart will typically state a percentage of income based on the number of children for whom support is to be paid. For example, the chart may indicate that the child support amount is 20% of the payor's income for one child, 31% for two children, and so on.

YOUR CHILD SUPPORT AMOUNT

Now that you have determined what minimum guideline amount would be acceptable in your state, you and the other parent should consider what additional amounts, if any, you believe would be best applied to your child's support.

For example, every year the federal government publishes an annual estimate of how much it costs for both parents who live together to raise a child. Using figures for 2005, researchers have shown that on average, it costs around $7,000 every year to raise a child when the family income is around $40,000. When the family income is between $43,000 and $70,000, expenditures for raising a child increase to about $10,500. The figures increase in households with more than one child. Overall, housing accounts for the biggest share of the expense—about 35% of the total, followed by food (15%–20%), and then transportation (15%).

Recently, economists compared state guidelines to 2004 estimates of child-rearing costs and found that nearly half of states' guideline amounts fell below the actual costs to raise a child. (Jane c. Venohr & Tracy E. Griffith, *Child Support Guidelines: Issues & Reviews*, 43 Fam. Ct. Rev. 415, 422-23 (July 2005).)

Some states have raised their guideline amounts. You can compare your state's current guideline amounts to the annual United States Department of Agriculture annual expenditure amounts, or simply compute the cost of raising your own child on a monthly basis. Check to see how it compares to the minimum guideline amount for a truer picture of how much you expend on child-related costs.

Below the Guideline Amount

If exceptional circumstances exist, you may determine that an amount lower than the guidelines is appropriate. State factors vary, and you will probably need to explain to a judge or hearing officer why you have agreed to support below the guideline amount.

Example:

In California, a court will approve the parties' agreement for child support that is below the guidelines only if all four of the following conditions are met.

1. They are fully informed of their rights concerning child support.

2. The order is being agreed to without coercion or duress.

3. The agreement is in the best interests of the children involved.

4. The needs of the children will be adequately met by the stipulated amount.

WRITING YOUR AGREEMENT

Once you have worked through the relevant issues and determined that your agreement meets, exceeds, or is permitted to be less than the guideline amounts, begin writing. (see form 9, p.222.)

Make sure your written agreement covers:

- ✪ how much the payment will be;

- ✪ the duration of the child support order;

- ✪ when and how child support will be paid;

- ✪ who is responsible for health care coverage;

- ✪ any special conditions of support; and,

- ✪ who will take the tax credit or exemption.

The agreement should indicate that you both are fully aware of your obligations under your state's guidelines. For example, you might state the following.

> Child support will be set in accordance with the State of [your home state] guidelines. We know that the amount agreed to is the presumptively correct amount under state guidelines. We know we can pay more, but we cannot pay less without approval from the court.

DURATION OF THE ORDER

The length of the child support order depends on the agreement of the parties or the terms ordered by the court. Many orders expire when the child reaches 18 (the age of majority). Parents may agree that they will support a child after he or she reaches the age of majority. This usually arises when the parents are in agreement that the child becomes self-supporting.

Unless some kind of agreement is made beyond the period of time that a child reaches the age of majority, the court usually will not order such support. Sometimes, though, there is a state law that requires the parents to support their child longer. For example, Maryland permits an order of support for an adult child where the child is "exceptional," such as where the child has emotional problems, and Florida parents of a disabled 50-year-old were ordered to pay lifelong support on their child.

An example of the language to express the duration of a support agreement follows.

> We further agree that child support shall be paid until our child reaches the age of eighteen (18) (or nineteen (19) if still in high school), dies, marries, or joins the military. We also agree that we will review our child's progress and encourage our child to go on to college or technical school as his or her interests and abilities permit, and we agree to contribute sums towards our child's education beyond high school to the extent our financial situation reasonably permits.

PAYMENTS

Although historically, the child support order required the payments be made directly to the other parent, this has proven to be problematic and made enforcement difficult. Instead, some states require that payments be made through the court clerk's office; however, federal regulations now require a centralized location to process payments, and most states have implemented this change.

An agreement should include when and how child support shall be paid. For example, the parents might agree to the following.

> Child support shall be paid by [name] on the fifteenth of every month to the state central registry, beginning on July 15, 2007.

Income Withholding

Automatic withholding of child support from the paying parent's income is one of the simplest ways to pay child support. If the paying parent is employed, the child support is withheld when the employer makes out the payroll, and is sent to the support collection agency designated in a court order. The funds are then dispersed by the agency according to state and federal laws.

Income withholding is not limited to salary and wages.

Example:
Nebraska's income withholding law permits the withholding of nearly any kind of income, including salaries or wages, unemployment and workers' compensation, investment funds, and retirement plans.

Electronic Funds Transfer

While some parents pay their child support directly by check, many states now offer an automatic payment option, known as *electronic funds transfer* (EFT). The electronic funds transfer automatically deducts the child support from a checking or savings account. This saves time preparing payments, saves money on postage and check fees, and ensures that payments cannot get lost or delayed in the mail.

In some states, automated options exist for receiving the child support. If you are entitled to child support that is paid to you through a support collection agency, you may be able to use a direct deposit method for your child support payments. Using direct deposit provides quicker access to the support funds, and your check cannot be delayed in the mail, lost, or stolen. In these states, all that is needed is for you to have a checking or savings account. The clerk of the court or the child support registry will electronically deposit your funds into your account.

Schedule of Payments   Most states require payments to be in dollar amounts. This makes it easier to use orders for withholding and also makes past-due calculations easier. Therefore, an agreement should use fixed dollar amounts.

HEALTH CARE

It should be clear in any agreement who is responsible for providing health care coverage for the child.

> It is agreed that [name] can obtain suitable health care coverage through an employer at the most reasonable cost. Therefore, the parties agree that health care coverage shall be provided by [name]. For out-of-pocket health care costs above those covered by insurance, the parties agree to prorate the expenses according to the state guideline percentage of support income, which is currently sixty percent (60%) for [name] and forty percent (40%) for [name]. These payments shall be made within thirty (30) days of the billing or insurance notice of payment due, whichever comes last. Both parties agree to promptly execute and deliver any documents to ensure timely payment of insurance claims. In the event that the paying party fails to maintain insurance, that party agrees to pay all health care expenses of the child.

LIFE INSURANCE

As security for future support, parents may agree to maintain life insurance on themselves, naming their child the beneficiary. The parties might agree as follows.

During the existence of the child support order, both [name] and [name] will obtain and maintain suitable life insurance coverage in the amount of ____. Both parties further agree that the child will be named the beneficiary of such policies. Each party will provide the other with a copy of the policy and annual proof of payment of the premiums.

TAX EXEMPTION

Who takes the dependent tax exemption should be covered in any agreement. For example, typical language might be as follows.

For income tax purposes, [name] can claim the child as an income tax exemption in odd-numbered years beginning with the year 2007, and [name] can claim the child as an income tax exemption in even-numbered years beginning with the year 2008. Both parties agree to cooperate in the timely signing and filing of any required or necessary revenue forms to accomplish this purpose.

SAMPLE

COMBINED INCOME CHILD SUPPORT WORKSHEET

	Parent	Parent	Combined
1. Total Monthly GROSS Income:	_____	_____	_____

Less Monthly Deductions (if your state uses gross income method, ignore deductions and carry line 1 amounts to line 2):

	Parent	Parent	Combined
Taxes	_____	_____	
FICA (Social Security)	_____	_____	
Health Insurance	_____	_____	
Mandatory Retirement	_____	_____	
Prior Child Support Order	_____	_____	
Total Deductions:	_____	_____	

2. Monthly NET/GROSS Income (subtract Total Deductions from line 1 amounts; if your state uses the gross income method, these will be the same amounts as on line 1): _____ _____

3. Monthly COMBINED Income (add line 2 incomes): _____

4. Each parent's percentage (divide each parent's line 2 amount by the line 3 combined income amount): _____ _____

5. Monthly Support Guideline Amount (from your state's guidelines): _____

6. Each parent's share (multiply line 5 by each parent's line 4 percentage): _____ _____

NOTE: *You may have other additions or deductions to income as permitted by your state.*

SAMPLE

PERCENTAGE OF INCOME CHILD SUPPORT WORKSHEET

Paying Parent

1. Total Monthly GROSS Income: _____

   Less Monthly Deductions (if your state uses
   the gross income method, ignore deductions
   and carry line 1 amount to line 2):

       Taxes   _____

       FICA (Social Security)   _____

       Health Insurance   _____

       Mandatory Retirement   _____

       Prior Child Support Order   _____

   Total Deductions: _____

2. Monthly NET/GROSS Income (subtract Total
   Deductions from the line 1 amount; if your state
   uses the gross income method, this will be
   the same amount as on line 1):   _____

3. Monthly Child Support Amount (find the
   percentage due according to your state guidelines,
   and multiply line 2 by that percentage):   _____

NOTE: *You may have other additions or deductions to income as permitted by your state.*

The Child Support Case

You may be filing for child support as part of your divorce case (or legal separation or annulment case), as part of an independent custody case, or as an independent case for child support alone. If you have worked out an agreement, you can include that agreement in your divorce settlement agreement and judgment, in your child custody/visitation agreement and order, or as an agreement and order in your independent child support case.

If you have no agreement and handle your own case, you will need to proceed with the legal process to have a judge issue a support order. This means that you will need to fill out, serve, and file several court forms. For example, to get support, you must know where the other parent lives or works. This will allow you to properly notify the other parent that you are seeking child support and to easily obtain necessary income information about the other parent in order to get an appropriate child support amount determined. Basically, you will need to supply the judge with information about your financial situation, the other parent's financial situation, and your child's financial needs.

NOTE: *If you are seeking a child support order as part of an independent case, you will need to file a complaint to establish parentage (if necessary). (See pages 136–137 for more information about establishing parentage.)*

GATHERING FINANCIAL INFORMATION

Every state requires that both parties disclose certain financial information to properly determine the amount of child support. Although the financial information relates directly to the determination of child support, states may also require such information to be provided in connection with filing a petition for custody or visitation. This will often be in the form of a **FINANCIAL AFFIDAVIT**. (see form 8, p.217.)

Therefore, in addition to the information you gathered about the other parent and your child in preparing your case (see Chapter 5), you should obtain financial information (as discussed below) about yourself and the other parent.

Employment

To obtain a complete picture of the earning capacity of a parent, courts consider the employment pattern of a parent for some period of time prior to the filing of the petition—usually three to five years. Financial employment information should include:

- the name and address of the parent's employer(s) for the past three years;

- the type and hours of employment;

- the parent's gross and net salary or wages per month, and upon what the deductions are based; and,

- whether there are any other employment benefits (e.g., commissions, bonuses, profit sharing, stock purchase, insurance, or retirement plans).

Other Income Sources

To properly measure the expenses of a parent and the available resources, many states consider whether there are other adults in the parent's household who are available to contribute to living expenses. Also, child support received under a prior court order may be considered, and in some states, child support paid by a parent for a prior child will be deducted as an adjustment to income. Some states also consider the child's available resources and the source of that income. Information to gather includes:

- child support received form other relationships;

- income of other adults in the parent's home;

- available cash (e.g., bank deposits, stocks, bonds, cash value of life insurance policies); and,

- the child's income.

Monthly Expense Information

Child support guidelines are premised on a recognition that a parent has certain living and personal expenses. This information is required to establish whether there is a basis for an increase or decrease in the support amount called for by the application of guidelines. The standard categories of expenses found in various states' child support worksheets, which are required to be completed in every state, include:

- housing (rent, mortgage payments, property taxes, homeowner's insurance);

- utilities (electric, gas, water, sewer, garbage collection, telephone, cable television, etc.);

- food and supplies (paper, tobacco, pets, groceries, meals eaten out);

- child expenses (clothing, school tuition and expenses, tutoring, health allowances, recreation, day care, and baby-sitting);

- transportation costs (car payments, insurance, license fees, gas, oil, routine maintenance, parking, and public transportation);

- health care (insurance premiums, uninsured medical, dental, orthodontic, and optical expenses); and,

- personal expenses (clothing, personal care, recreation, education, gifts, and other insurance costs).

FILING FOR CHILD SUPPORT

A parent (or other eligible custodian for a child) may file for child support in the local courts, on his or her own, or through an attorney. Some states allow certain child support orders to be established administratively by a state agency designated by law to do so.

All states have a state-run child support enforcement program. These agencies are listed in Appendix A. These programs may provide the following services:

- location of absent parents;

- establishment of paternity;

- establishment and modification of support orders;

- enforcement of support orders;

- establishment and modification of medical support orders; and,

- the collection and distribution of support payments.

A state's child support enforcement agency can also arrange child support orders. This is beneficial because it is faster than going to court.

While these services are available to all families regardless of their financial status, many of the clients are aid-dependent families, and the child support payments collected go toward reimbursement of the assistance benefits paid to the families. To request child support services, an individual may apply through a local child support agency.

In many cases, unless the parent receives public assistance, there will be a fee for filing a petition. Some states do not charge for administrative filings, while others permit the fee to be paid over time. States also permit a parent to request a waiver of fees by filing a special request explaining why he or she cannot pay the fees and costs of maintaining the case. You can obtain filing fee information from your local court clerk's office or child support agency. If you believe you are eligible for a deferral or waiver of the filing fees, these agencies will also have the necessary forms.

If you are filing an independent case for child support, you will need the same basic information as you would in preparing for a custody case. This is because custody will necessarily be decided at the time of ordering the child support. (see Chapter 4.) Most states have **CHILD SUPPORT CALCULATION WORKSHEETS** to follow in preparing for your child support case. (see form 9, p.222.)

When you have completed the necessary worksheets and court- or agency-required forms, you may file them and arrange for service on the other parent. This is the same procedure as you would use in a custody filing. (see Chapter 5.)

FINDING AND NOTIFYING A PARENT

In order to obtain an order for support, the child's parent must be notified and has a right to appear in court and answer the petition. Notifying the parent requires information on where the parent lives or works. If you do not know the current address or employer for the other parent, the easiest way to find a person is through his or her Social Security number, although names and addresses of friends and relatives, past employers, banks, utility companies, clubs, and organizations may also be helpful.

If you have sought assistance from your local child support enforcement agency, it may also have resources that can assist in finding the other parent. State child support enforcement agencies have *State Parent Locator Service* (SPLS) facilities that can help find the absent parent. The SPLS will use the parent's Social Security number to check records of other agencies within your state, such as the motor vehicle registration agencies, unemployment insurance, income tax, and prison or jail facilities in an effort to find the absent parent. They can also request information from utility companies, schools, employers, post offices, and more.

Out-of-State Parent   The most difficult child support cases are those in which the parent who has been ordered to pay child support lives in one state and the child and the custodial parent live in another. All states provide methods to get child support in these cases. Federal law requires the state enforcement agencies to cooperate with each other in handling requests for assistance under the *Uniform Interstate Family Support Act* (UIFSA). All states have adopted UIFSA laws substantially similar to the federal model, and rely heavily on them for pursuing enforcement in other states. The Uniform Interstate Family Support Act provides extended powers to states to reach beyond their own state lines for the establishment of support orders. All states have a *Central Registry* to receive incoming interstate child support cases, review them to make sure that the information given is complete, distribute them to the right local office, and reply to status inquiries from child support offices in other states.

If the absent parent has moved out of state, the state can ask the *Federal Parent Locator Service* (FPLS) for assistance. The FPLS will search the records of the Internal Revenue Service (IRS), Social Security Administration, Department of Veterans Affairs, and state unemployment agencies, among others, to search for current address or employment information on the absent parent.

Most child support enforcement agencies have a very high demand for their services, so they have to set priorities among the cases they receive. Interstate cases can take several months to complete. In fact, it can take nine months or longer for a custodial parent to receive support from an out-of-state parent. Even once the parent is located and notified, if a hearing is necessary, it may take more time to get a court date.

ESTABLISHING PARENTAGE (IF NECESSARY)

Parentage must be legally recognized in order to get a support order. Usually, identifying a biological mother is easy, and in a traditional marriage, the child is presumed to be the husband's child.

However, more than one million children are born outside of marriage every year. When a man and a woman are not married, paternity must be established so that the father gains certain rights to his child, and the child also gains certain rights. Among these may be the right to inherit from the father, the right to medical and life insurance benefits, and the right to certain federal benefits, such as Social Security and veteran's benefits.

Under welfare reform laws enacted in 1996, it is easier and faster than before to establish paternity. The father may acknowledge that he is the child's father in order for a child support order to be entered. When the child is born in a hospital, the father can acknowledge paternity right there. Many fathers voluntarily acknowledge paternity.

If the father does not voluntarily acknowledge paternity, the issue must be proven in court. Each state provides for the requirements to establish that the person is the parent of the child.

All states provide for some presumptions of paternity. For example, if a child is born during a marriage, that child is presumed to be the child of the husband and wife. If the husband believes that he is not the father, he can challenge this presumption. Genetic (DNA) testing can be done to determine whether he is the father.

Most states require that paternity be established by a *preponderance of the evidence*, meaning that paternity (or lack of paternity) is more likely than not. Putting this standard in terms of numbers, it means that there has to be a 51% weight to the evidence to find paternity. Some states insist on a higher *clear and convincing* standard, which is a tougher standard to meet than proof by a preponderance of the evidence.

Whatever the burden of proof on a person asserting or denying paternity, DNA testing may make these distinctions irrelevant. The father, mother, and child can be required to submit to genetic tests. The results are highly accurate. With proper testing, most cases are decided on scientific evidence that is nearly always accurate.

FOLLOWING COURT PROCEDURES

Once the parent has been notified (and if necessary, paternity has been established), the next issue is how much support should be awarded. Answering this question requires the court to consider the financial information forms required to be filed in child support cases, and may require testimony from the parents and others, including experts, regarding the contested income and expenses presented.

Seeking a Temporary Order of Support

The court (or administrative agency, if permitted in your state) in which you file the application or petition for child support can enter a temporary order of child support. Whether support will be granted temporarily depends on the needs of the parent seeking that support during the time the case is pending. There will also be consideration given to whether the other parent has the ability to pay the support.

Requesting a temporary order of child support is made by a formal request to the court. The papers filed should indicate the financial needs of the child or children. You need to file a **MOTION FOR TEMPORARY RELIEF**. (see form 7, p.215.) An **ORDER FOR TEMPORARY RELIEF** will be issued by the judge. (see form 10, p.225.)

Security for Payment

Where the parties have not agreed on a support amount, a court may order security for payment of a child support order. This usually takes form in the establishment or maintenance of a life insurance policy or the creation of a trust for the children. Some states mandate that this be done.

Also, the court may order that the parent who pays support obtain a life insurance policy on him- or herself to protect the payment plan. In some states, a child support order may automatically create a lien on the paying parent's property.

Example:

The court could order a lien against the real estate of the parent who owes support, so that if support remained unpaid, the property could be sold to pay the lien.

A court can also order a parent to obtain required health care coverage through a special order called a *qualified medical child support order*. This requires that the employer's group health care plan provide coverage for a child. The employer can charge the parent for any premiums to carry out this order.

If the paying parent has a pension or retirement plan at work, the court can issue a *qualified domestic relations order*. This orders the employer to add the child on as a payee of the plan as security for the child support order.

A court may also protect the best interests of the child by setting aside a part of either jointly held or individually held property of the parents in a separate trust or fund to pay for the support, education, and welfare of a minor child or dependent child. This usually means that either the parent is ordered to hold property *in trust* or actually set up a trust account for the child.

RESPONDING TO A PETITION FOR CHILD SUPPORT

Every state has statutes of limitations that govern the period within which a case may be filed. For example, a state may require that a child support case must be filed before the child reaches the age of 18. Therefore, check to be sure that the petition covers an eligible child.

Next, to pay child support, you must be found to be the legal parent of the child in question. If you believe you are not the parent, you may raise it as a defense against a request for child support.

If you are the parent of the child, and you seek to have custody, you may wish to contest child support and file a *counterclaim* for custody and request child support of your own. You may instead wish to challenge the child support amount requested on the basis that it is the product of incorrect income information, adjustments, or expense items. States' guideline amounts may be adjusted upward or downward based on a number of factors.

Failure to obtain the agreed-upon (or ordered) visitation is not a defense to avoid paying child support.

Finally, if you agree that child support is due to your child, you will answer the petition and provide your own financial affidavit to the court for review, so a complete picture of the child's needs and the parent's resources can then be evaluated, and a proper child support award can be determined.

Default   All states require the respondent (who may also be called a *defendant*) to respond within a certain time limit to the notice of the child support petition. If the defendant fails to respond, he or she can be *defaulted*, which means that the case proceeds without them.

In such cases, courts rely heavily on the presumptions of the guideline amounts, but will permit the parent who filed the petition to introduce evidence of additional need. The support amount may accordingly be higher than the guidelines.

Modification, Termination, and Appeal

A child custody agreement or order is intended to last as long as the child needs a caretaker. Parties can agree to a change of custody or visitation, but because the court has jurisdiction, it must be put in writing and filed in the proper court.

MODIFICATION

Courts generally agree that the less disruption in the child's schedule and environment, the better, so they are reluctant to change custody or visitation orders. However, circumstances change, and sometimes these circumstances lead to a request by a parent to modify or change the custody or visitation order. This is why it is said that a child custody or visitation order is never truly final.

Sometimes the original order of custody or visitation is too uncertain. The parties may interpret it differently, which can lead to frequent disputes. In such a case, the court might modify the order to specify the details of the custody and visitation.

Jurisdiction   To modify an order, a parent may return to the same court that entered the original order. It is not unusual for one parent to have moved, and that parent may seek a modification in his or her new home state.

The UCCJA and UCCJEA

The *Uniform Child Custody Jurisdiction Act* (UCCJA) applies not only to initial custody orders, but also to modifications between parties from different states. The goal of the UCCJA in modification issues is to reduce the chances that two states will enter conflicting orders. Its successor, the *Uniform Child Custody Jurisdiction and Enforcement Act* (UCCJEA), is being used in most states. Check with your local court clerk to see which form you need.

The Limits

To obtain stability for a child, some states prohibit parents from seeking changes to their custody and visitation orders before some specified period of time. In Illinois, for example, parties must wait two years before returning to a court seeking modification unless there are substantial changes in circumstances that show that the child's current environment endangers his or her well-being.

A court will generally not revisit the facts that led to the initial order of custody or visitation. The parent seeking the change will have to present facts that show there has been a substantial change of circumstances since the order was issued, and that the requested change in custody or visitation will be in the best interests of the child.

Like most other determinations involving a child, there is no single standard by which it can be determined when enough circumstances have changed to make it substantial. The court will be guided by what is in the best interests of the child. The simplest way to think about it is to recognize that the measure of what is *substantial* will be looked at through the effect that the change in circumstances has on the child—not the effect on the parent.

Example:

Winning the lottery will not amount to a sufficient change of circumstances to deprive the nonwinning parent of custody. If that nonwinning parent needs more funds to properly care for the child, the proper remedy would be to seek an increase in child support—not a modification of custody or visitation.

Typical reasons for seeking a change are:

- ✪ a change in income or employment status;

- ✪ extraordinary medical expenses;

- ✪ a change in family size; or,

- ✪ a change in shared parental responsibilities.

It is usually not enough to show that the visiting parent does not always exercise his or her visitation with the child, or that the child has been disappointed on holidays or special occasions, unless these occurrences have a substantial negative impact on the child.

Remarriage   The remarriage of a parent alone is not enough to change custody or visitation. It may, however, be a factor that, when combined with other factors, results in the requested change. Often, with a remarriage comes a move into a new home. This may result in the merging of new family members, the increased expenses of the new family, or increased income. The change in home life of the child may have an effect on the request to modify custody or visitation. For example, the attitude of the new stepparent, the treatment of the child in the new home, or the new environment or religious upbringing that the child may experience are all factors that a court may examine. Also, the relocation often involved in a remarriage of the custodial parent may result in difficulty for the noncustodial parent to visit the child.

Moving   Once a custody or visitation case has been filed in a court, a parent who wishes to move with the child to another state, or even to a distant point within the state, must have permission of the court to do so. A court will grant permission only if it is in the best interests of the child to do so.

The laws of each state vary considerably on the specific requirements that must be shown before a move will be granted. In California, for example, as of 2004, legislation affirms court rulings that make it clear that a parent with custody is not required to show that it is necessary to move as long as it is not prejudicial to the child's welfare. (Cal. Fam. Code, Sec. 750.) In Alabama, the parent with the right to establish principal residence of the child must provide notice of a proposal to move, and include a statement of reasons for the proposal, as the state law currently presumes that any change of principal residence is not in the best interests of a child, and the person seeking to move must overcome that presumption. (ALA. Code, Sec. 30-3-150.) Illinois passed a law in 2003 that allows a court to prohibit an unmarried parent from removing the child from the state while custody and visitation are being decided, and requires a court to consider the impact of the denial on the party seeking to move the child. (750 ILCS 45/13.5.) Louisiana puts the burden on the parent seeking to move to show that it is in the best interest of the child, and requires consideration of whether a proposed move is necessary to improve the employment and economic circumstances of the parent seeking to move the child out of state. (La. Rev. Stat., Sec. 9:355.12.)

If the noncustodial parent is moving, special provisions for visitation will need to be made. The court can also order the parent who wishes to move to pay for transportation costs and to post a bond to the court to secure the return of the child.

Travel   A parent must obtain the court's or the other parent's permission to even take the child out of state temporarily on a vacation.

Example:

Some states now require the vacationing parent to provide the other parent with information on where the child can be reached during the vacation or other absence from the state, as well as the dates of the proposed absence, before the child can leave.

Misconduct by a Parent   If the parent with custody engages in a pattern of disrupting the child's relationship with the visiting parent or otherwise interfering with visitation, this may result in a request for a transfer of custody. Similarly, if the visiting parent interferes with the custodial parent's relationship with the child, this can result in a denial or limitation of visitation.

Courts may first try to achieve the desired result of stopping the interference or alienation of the child through other methods, such as warning the parent or holding the parent in contempt of court. However, if there is a strong pattern of disrespect and even hatred shown, the court may change custody or visitation on the grounds that it is in the best interests of the child to do so.

Abandonment   Sometimes a parent with custody will give the child to another person, such as the child's grandparent, to raise. A temporary arrangement will usually not result in any kind of custody change, but if the child is not returned to the parent within a reasonable amount of time, custody may be transferred to the visiting parent.

Example:

If the parent with custody has a chance to get a job in another city, it may be okay to have the child finish the remaining few months of the school year with the grandparents. However, if the parent with custody is not looking for a place to live with the child and apparently intends to leave the child with the grandparents indefinitely, the visiting parent's request for a change of custody may be granted.

Court Order Required   Even if the parties agree to a change of custody or visitation, it will only be binding once a court has approved it. The ultimate decision to grant a request for a change in custody or visitation rests with the judge. Ordinarily, the court can change custody or visitation in the following situations.

- The parties have agreed to the change of custody.

- The child has been integrated into the home of the visiting parent who is requesting the change with the permission of the parent with custody.

- The child's present home environment is dangerous to his or her health, and a change of environment is in the child's best interests.

Filing for a Change in Custody or Visitation

To notify the other parent, file a motion or **Petition to Modify Judgment** with the court. (see form 26, p.262.) You will need to explain why the change is sought. This will be done either in the petition itself or in a separate affidavit, depending upon the practice in your state. The parent filing the request must notify the other parent, because in the absence of an emergency, a change of custody or visitation will not be made without proper notice, giving the other parent an opportunity to be heard. Different courts require different levels of notice. Notice by publication may be permitted when the parent does not know, and cannot find out, where the other parent lives.

The court will hold a hearing. If a parent objects to the request, a full trial may be held in which both parents may have to present witnesses and put on evidence. The parent who requests the change has the burden to prove how the circumstances have substantially changed since the child custody order was entered.

As can be seen, the request to change custody or modify visitation is a very serious matter, and is treated by the courts as seriously as the initial grant of custody or visitation.

While an existing child support order is always subject to modification, it is important to recognize that modifications are not usually automatic. Each parent may seek either an upward or downward modification. However, to do so requires the parent seeking the modification to return to a court (or administrative agency, if permitted by your state) and obtain a new child support order.

In order to obtain some stability, most states require some period of time to pass (two or three years is common) or that the person seeking the modification show a substantial change in circumstances that warrants a review of the child support order.

Example 1:
In Washington, a child support order must be at least twelve months old before a party may request a modification.

Example 2:

In Virginia, reasons for requesting a review include: if there is a change in the gross income or employment status of either parent; if an order needs to be amended because medical support is not a part of the current support order; if extraordinary medical expenses for the child occur; and, if a change in the family's size occurs.

Substantial Changes in Circumstances

In most states, it will be considered a substantial or significant change in circumstances if the guidelines have changed significantly. That is, if the guidelines amount at the time the order was entered is substantially different than the amount that would be due under the current guidelines.

In Arizona and Florida, for example, the law requires the person seeking the modification to show that an estimation of his or her current circumstances would result in a variance of 15% or more from the existing amount. In Florida, the 15% must equal at least a $50 difference. In Vermont, the change required for a modification of child support must be a "real, substantial and unanticipated change in circumstances," and must result in a change of at least 10% between the current order and the amount calculated under the child support guidelines (not a 10% change in income).

Some states, such as Arizona, permit a simplified proceeding. To show this variation, a parent is required to provide the court with a document proving the variance. The document will then be served upon the other parent. If no hearing is requested by the other parent, a court can simply review the request and enter the change in the order. If the matter is contested, there will be a hearing on the issue of the variance.

In Texas, only a court can modify child support—it cannot be done by agreement of the parties. Grounds for a modification include either 1) a material and substantial change in the circumstances of a child or the parent, or 2) the passage of at least three years since the last child support order, and under the current child support guidelines, the previously ordered monthly payment would change by at least 20% or $100.

In most states, obtaining a modification requires:

- ✪ acquiring a certified copy of the current support order (check with your court clerk);

- ✪ completing the necessary petition or form application for a modification;

- ✪ paying a filing fee (unless waived); and,

- ✪ filing the forms with the child support agency or a court.

Past-Due Support   Modification of past-due child support is not permitted by federal law. Modification can only be for future payments, so if a significant change in circumstances prevents payment of support, you must file your documents seeking a downward modification (or suspension) of support as soon as possible.

Remarriage   The second marriage of a parent will not have an impact on a child support order, but new obligations to children will often result in that parent seeking modification of the order. The traditional view was that your child should not have support reduced because you decide to take on the obligations for a new family; however, many state guidelines now factor in obligations for such subsequent children.

Change of Job   The change in employment of a parent may be considered for a modification of future child support. However, if unemployment or underemployment results from an intentional choice or willfulness of the parent, the court may refuse to grant such a request.

Change of Custody   A change in the parenting of a child will often be grounds for modification of a child support order. Keep in mind, however, that this is not automatic. The child support order will not be changeable until your petition to modify it is filed with the appropriate agency or clerk of the court.

TERMINATION

Child custody, visitation, and support orders typically terminate when the child reaches the age of majority (usually 18). However, many states have laws that authorize a court to continue child support for a limited period of time past the age of majority (usually until age 19), as long as the child is enrolled as a full-time high school student. A few states have statutes that authorize the court to continue child support until the child graduates from college. There have been cases where a court ordered the payment of graduate school; however, these situations are not common. The parties may agree to pay for the child's support for higher educational purposes or for some other reason until a specified event or date.

Child's Marriage

A child's marriage operates as an emancipation event, so even if the child is still considered a minor under the law, the court orders will terminate upon marriage.

Child's Military Service

A child's enlisting in the military is usually seen as an emancipation event, even if the child is still a minor under the law. A child entering the military service operates to terminate a child custody, visitation, and support order in most states.

If there is more than one child covered by a support order, the emancipation of one child will proportionately reduce the order in most states. The reduction occurs automatically. However, in some states, the order is not reduced unless the parent responsible for payment seeks a reduction.

Death of a Parent

Although in some states, the power to make further custody orders ends with the death of a parent, in others, a court still has power to change the order.

In all states, the death of a parent will not excuse any past-due child support, and increasingly, the death of a parent will not terminate the child support order. Parties may agree to terminate support in the event of the death of a parent, upon payment of a lump sum (such as through the purchase of a life insurance policy naming the child as beneficiary). Even if the order does not terminate, the death of the party owing support will usually be grounds for seeking a modification of the order.

Example:
Out of the deceased parent's estate, the amount calculated to be due for support may be determined and converted into a lump-sum payment. If the deceased parent owes past due-child support, a claim can also be made against that parent's estate.

Remarriage   Remarriage of a parent is not a factor that, by itself, will operate to terminate a child custody order.

Adoption   The adoption of the child by the new spouse of the custodial parent usually operates to terminate a child support order. However, this will not usually relieve the paying parent of the obligation for any past-due support.

APPEAL

Either party to the case may file *posttrial proceedings* seeking to change the decision in the case. Every state has a system of courts designed to hear appeals. No testimony is taken in the appellate process. The court decides the appeal based on the objections that are filed as well as the records and transcript of the trial court. Some states, like Illinois, expedite appeals in child custody cases. If a serious mistake was made, the judgment can be overturned and the case sent back for a retrial.

Although many appeals may be taken in family law cases, reversals are rare. This is because the appellate court will uphold the trial judge's decision unless there has been an *abuse of discretion* or a serious error in applying the law. This makes sense, because it is the trial judge who has (perhaps) interviewed the child, listened to the parents, and heard the experts testify. For example, if the child support amount is within the guidelines, the trial court has the discretion to make an award that is just and equitable.

An appeals court simply reads the arguments of the parties, reviews the record of the proceedings in the trial court, and decides if a significant error was made. Since the factors and guidelines are very broad, it is hard to prove an abuse of discretion in most cases.

THE FUTURE

Now that you have read and familiarized yourself with the law and procedures involved in pursuing orders concerning the parenting of a child and the guideline factors courts will apply in determining child support, you should return to the beginning chapters of this book and begin the process of brainstorming your choices. This way, you increase the likelihood that an agreement can be reached with the other parent concerning parental responsibilities. The decisions you make in this area are critical and may last decades. Armed with the necessary legal information, think carefully about your options and always weigh your decisions against the best interests of your child.

Glossary

A

affidavit.   A statement of facts made in writing under oath before an authorized person, such as a notary public, that the contents of the document are true to the best of his or her knowledge.

alternative dispute resolution.   A manner to resolve disputes outside of or apart from the court system. Arbitration and mediation are two common techniques.

B

best interests standard.   The standard applied to the determination of custody, visitation, or parenting time used in all states. This standard makes certain presumptions about what is best for a child, and examines the child's environment against certain factors set out in the relevant state's code.

C

closing argument.   The final summation of the evidence by a party.

cross-examination.   The opportunity of a party to ask leading questions of the witness put on by the other party in order to clarify, limit, or impeach that witness' testimony before a court.

custody.   A parent's right to have the care, control, and responsibility for his or her child's upbringing. In some cases, third parties, such as other family members or psychological parents, may have custody over a child by court order.

D

decree.   An order that has the force of law. This may also be called a judgment.

de facto parent.   A nonparent who has become the primary caregiver for a child.

deposition.   Part of the discovery process in a case, a deposition is comprised of questions asked and answers given by a witness in a case who is under oath. The questioning is done by the opposing attorney, and is not in a courtroom or under the supervision of a judge. The answers are recorded by a court reporter.

discovery.   This is the process by which the parties, formally or informally, exchange information about the case. It is done prior to trial and may include interrogatories, requests to admit facts, and depositions among other methods.

due diligence.   The exercise of reasonable efforts to complete a task, such as discovering the proper address in an attempt to serve papers on the opposing spouse.

G

guardian ad litem.   The person, usually an attorney, appointed by the court to watch out for the best interests of the child during the court case.

I

interrogatory.   One type of formal discovery in which questions are sent in writing to the opposing party and must be answered under oath.

J

joint custody.   This may include legal or physical custody situations where the parties share the responsibility for their child pursuant to court order or judgment.

joint legal custody.   This is one of two types of custody. Legal custody is the right to be involved in making decisions typically involved with being a parent, such as religious training, education, and medical care. Legal custody can be either sole or joint.

joint physical custody.   This is one of two types of custody. A parent who has physical custody lives most of the time with the child and makes daily care decisions during that time.

judgment.   A formal decision of a court. This may also be called a decree or the court's order.

M

motion.   A request to a court, often in writing, to obtain a ruling or order from the court.

N

notice.   The process by which the other party is notified of the filing of a document or the setting of a court date.

O

order.   A pronouncement of the judge. Orders may be temporary or permanent. If an order resolves all of the issues in a case, it is called a judgment or decree.

P

parenting schedule.   The details of the actual time that a parent (or person with the right to see the child) spends with the child. This may include significant dates like birthdays and holidays, as well as routine periods, such as every Tuesday.

parenting time.   As opposed to a legal concept of custody, parenting time designates the actual time that a party spends with his or her child. Some courts may think of this as physical custody or visitation.

paternity.   The determination that a male is the father of a child.

psychological parent.   The person who has developed a parentlike relationship with the child due to extensive care for the child. This might include a grandparent, stepparent, or foster parent.

R

retainer.   This is an agreed amount paid to an attorney in order to commence legal action. Depending on the agreement, the retainer may range from a few hundred to a few thousand dollars. The agreement will specify how the funds are to be used against the attorney's time in the case.

S

process of serving a person with notice that a lawsuit
inst him or her. Unless waived by the parties, service
ually done by a person authorized by the court like a
ss server.

ing.   A newer and perhaps more accurate term for
esponsibility of a child, this term seeks to recognize
ts play a significant role in the upbringing of a child,
does away with old notions that one parent has cus-
er has visitation.

The dividing of responsibilities for two or more
the parents. For example, in a split custody situation,
ke custody of Child A and the dad of Child B, with
parents (and the siblings) having visitation.

rt order that commands a person to appear in court
tified documents in court on a set date and time.

ourt-ordered right given to a parent (or another)
ustody to see and care for their child during specific

Sample, Filled-in Forms

This appendix contains some forms that have been completed for a fictional case in a fictional state. This will give you further assistance in preparing the forms for your state. Following, under the heading "Factual Scenario" are the basic facts of the case. Under the heading "Table of Forms" is a list of the forms that are included in this appendix, along with the page on which each form begins.

FACTUAL SCENARIO

Susan Smith and John Jones have a child, Carrie Smith, whose date of birth is June 20, 2003. For three years after Carrie was born, the couple lived together at 222 Main Street, in the City of Happytown, which is in Bliss County, in the State of Utopia. They never married. John, however, has never contested the fact that he is the father. He acknowledged paternity when Carrie was born and consented to have his name appear on the birth certificate. In May 2006, the couple's relationship began to deteriorate, and John moved into his own apartment at 1 Northwood Street, #3, Happytown, which he shares with two of his coworkers. Susan remains in the Main Street apartment with their daughter. Susan's sister has moved into the apartment with Susan and pays part of the expenses there. Both

Susan's and John's families live nearby and baby-sit frequently for Carrie. Although John contributed to Carrie's support from her birth, he has not paid any support since he moved out in May 2006, except for $200, which he gave to Susan for Carrie's birthday party in June.

Susan attends college part-time and works part-time as an administrative assistant, earning approximately $14,000 annually. John just secured a new job full-time as an entry-level computer technician for a large company. He earns approximately $28,000 annually, but potentially will see significant increases in his salary as he gains seniority with the company. Susan's health benefits are provided through the local college. John has health benefits through his employer, and Carrie has been insured on his policy.

In early July 2006, Susan decided to file a petition for custody and child support. In her petition, Susan seeks sole custody and child support, but when the case was referred for mandatory mediation, both parties agreed to joint legal custody, keeping primary physical custody with Susan and providing liberal parenting time for John. The state's guidelines are followed to establish child support. This example calculates the monthly support sum due for child support in a combined adjusted gross income state. The judgment incorporates the agreement of the parties.

NOTE: *Although Carrie's expenses are low, as she gets older, they can be expected to increase. Additionally, it is likely that both Susan's and John's income levels will change considerably as Susan completes her education and can seek full-time employment in her field and as John advances in his career. These changes should trigger a review and adjustment upon a request for modification.*

TABLE OF FORMS

FORM 1:   PETITION TO ESTABLISH PATERNITY, CUSTODY AND
          TIME-SHARING, AND FOR CHILD SUPPORT 162

FORM 2:   SUMMONS. 166

FORM 3:   RESPONSE TO PETITION TO ESTABLISH PATERNITY,
          CUSTODY AND TIME-SHARING,
          AND FOR CHILD SUPPORT 167

FORM 4:   UNIFORM CHILD CUSTODY JURISDICTION AND
          ENFORCEMENT ACT (UCCJEA) AFFIDAVIT 169

FORM 5:   CERTIFICATE OF SERVICE 172

FORM 6:   NOTICE OF HEARING 173

FORM 7:   MOTION FOR TEMPORARY RELIEF. 174

FORM 8:   FINANCIAL AFFIDAVIT 176

FORM 9:   CHILD SUPPORT CALCULATION WORKSHEET 181

FORM 10: ORDER FOR TEMPORARY RELIEF. 184

FORM 11: MOTION AND ORDER FOR REFERRAL TO MEDIATION 185

FORM 13: PARENTING PLAN (ALTERNATIVE B) 187

FORM 15: REQUEST FOR HEARING 191

FORM 16: FINAL JUDGMENT 192

IN THE CIRCUIT COURT
BLISS COUNTY, UTOPIA

SUSAN SMITH,   )
          Petitioner,   )
    v.   )   Case No. 06-12345
)
JOHN JONES,   )
          Respondent.   )

PETITION TO ESTABLISH PATERNITY, CUSTODY AND TIME-SHARING, AND FOR CHILD SUPPORT

NOW COMES _____, Petitioner, and states as follows:

1.   Petitioner is a resident of ____Bliss____County.

2.   ____Petitioner____ is the mother of the minor child(ren).

3.   ____Respondent____ is the father of the minor child(ren).

4.   The name, date of birth, and age of the minor child(ren) is/are

Name	Date of Birth	Age
CARRIE SMITH	JUNE 20, 2003	3

PATERNITY [Choose 1]

❑ 5.   Paternity has not been established.

☒ 5.   Paternity has been established by:

    ☒   Respondent has acknowledged his paternity of the minor child(ren) in writing filed with the Department of Vital Statistics in the state in which the child(ren) was/were born.

    ❑   Respondent has consented to paternity and is named as father on the minor child(ren)'s birth certificate.

    ❑   Paternity of the minor child(ren) has been established by blood tests.

    ☒   Respondent has openly held out the minor child(ren) as his natural child(ren) and established a personal, financial, or custodial relationship with the child(ren).

HOME STATE AND RESIDENCE OF CHILDREN

❑ 6. A completed declaration under the Uniform Child Custody Jurisdiction And Enforcement Act Affidavit is attached to this petition.

❑ 7. The number of minor child(ren) subject to this proceeding is __1__.

The name, place of birth, birth date, and sex of each child; the present address, periods of residence, and places where each child has lived within the past five (5) years; and the name, present address, and relationship to the child of each person with whom the child has lived during that time are:

THE FOLLOWING INFORMATION IS TRUE ABOUT CHILD # 1:

Child's Full Legal Name: __Carrie Smith__

Place of Birth: __Happytown, Utopia__ Date of Birth: __June 20, 2003__ Sex: __F__

Child's Residence for the past 5 years:

Dates (From/To)	Address (including city and state) where child lived	Name and present address	Relationship to child
Birth – present	222 Main Street, Happytown, Utopia	Petitioner Susan Smith, 222 Main Street, Happytown, Utopia	Mother
Birth – May, 2006	222 Main Street, Happytown, Utopia	Petitioner Susan Smith and Respondent John Jones	Mother & Father

CUSTODY OPTIONS [Choose 1]

❑ 8. The parties should be awarded joint legal custody of the minor child(ren), with primary physical custody in and periods of care and responsibility consistent with the best interests of the child(ren).

☒ 8. Petitioner should be awarded sole legal and physical custody of the child(ren) subject to the respondent's reasonable rights of visitation. Sole legal and physical custody is in the best interests of the minor child(ren) because:

Petitioner is the primary caretaker of the minor child, and can provide a stable, consistent residence for the child

CHILD SUPPORT

☒ 9. Child support should be set according to this state's support guidelines and Respondent should be ordered to pay child support the amount determined by the child support guidelines. A worksheet form and financial affidavit will be timely filed and served on respondent.

☒ 10. Petitioner requests temporary child support during the pendency of this case, in accordance with this state's child support guidelines.

☒ 11. Petitioner requests that child support be retroactive to the birth of the child(ren), and that the amount of child support be in accordance with this state's child support guidelines.

LIFE INSURANCE

☒ 12. Respondent should be ordered to purchase life insurance with a benefit amount of $ __25,000__ , naming Petitioner as trustee for the benefit of the minor child(ren) to pay the child support obligation upon the respondent's death.

MEDICAL INSURANCE

☒ 13. __Respondent_____ should provide health and dental insurance for the minor child(ren).

MEDICAL EXPENSES [Choose 1]

❑ 14. _____ should pay 100% of the minor child(ren)'s health and dental expenses not paid by insurance.

❑ 14. The parties should each pay one-half of the child(ren)'s health and dental expenses not paid by insurance.

☒ 14. The parties should pay the child(ren)'s health and dental expenses not paid by insurance in the income percentages shown on the child support worksheet.

SCIENTIFIC TESTING

☒ 15. Petitioner requests scientific paternity testing be ordered if Respondent denies paternity of the child(ren), with blood or other bodily tissue or fluid samples to be sent for testing to a qualified blood testing laboratory and DNA tests, HLA tests, and any other tests the testing facility recommends to be performed. Petitioner requests that court costs, scientific testing costs, and expert witness fees should be ordered to be paid by Respondent.

BIRTH RECORD

☒   16.   Upon determination of paternity, the Department of Vital Statistics should be ordered to change the birth record of the minor child(ren) to reflect the paternity as determined by this court.

WHEREFORE, Petitioner asks the Court to:
1.   Establish the paternity of the minor child(ren).
2.   Award child custody in accordance with this Petition.
3.   Order child support according to the Child Support Guidelines.
4.   Grant such other and further relief as the Court deems just and equitable.

RESPECTFULLY SUBMITTED:

Susan Smith
Signature of Petitioner
Print Name: Susan Smith
Address: 222 Main Street
    Happytown, Utopia
Telephone: (555) 444-4444

ACKNOWLEDGMENT

STATE OF ____UTOPIA____   )
) SS.
COUNTY OF ____BLISS____   )

I,____Susan Smith____, being first duly sworn upon my oath, depose and state that I am the Petitioner in the above-entitled cause. I have read the attached PETITION TO ESTABLISH PATERNITY, CUSTODY AND TIME-SHARING, AND FOR CHILD SUPPORT. I state that the contents thereof are true and correct, except to the matters stated on information and belief, and those matters I believe to be true.

Susan Smith
Signature of Petitioner

SUBSCRIBED AND SWORN TO before me on
this _15th_ day of ____July____, _2006_ .

C.U. Sine
NOTARY PUBLIC
My Commission Expires: ____May 5, 2008____

IN THE CIRCUIT COURT
BLISS COUNTY, UTOPIA

SUSAN SMITH,   )
          Petitioner,   )
    v.   )   Case No. _06-12345_____
)
JOHN JONES,   )
          Respondent.   )

SUMMONS

TO THE RESPONDENT:

    Name of Respondent: _____John Johnes_____

    Address: _____16 Northwood Street, #3, Happytown, Utopia_____

To the Officer: This summons must be served by the Officer or other person to whom it was given for service, with the endorsement of service within 30 days after its date.

To the respondent: You are summoned and required to file an answer to the complaint in this case, a copy of which is attached to this summons. You must answer or otherwise respond within _30_ days after service of this summons. If you fail to do so, a judgment of default may be entered against you for the relief requested in the complaint.

ISSUED this ___15___ day of _____July_____, __2006__

                     *John R. Clerk*_____

                     Clerk of the District Court

                     By _____Clerk_____

IN THE CIRCUIT COURT
BLISS COUNTY, UTOPIA

SUSAN SMITH,   )
                    Petitioner,   )
        v.   )   Case No. 06-12345
)
JOHN JONES,   )
                    Respondent.   )

RESPONSE TO PETITION TO ESTABLISH PATERNITY, CUSTODY AND TIME-SHARING, AND FOR CHILD SUPPORT

I, _____JOHN JONES_____, Respondent, herein certify that the following information is true:

1.   I admit the allegations contained in the following numbered paragraphs in the Petition *{indicate paragraph number(s)}*: _____1-7, 14, 16_____
_____.

2.   I deny the allegations contained in the following numbered paragraphs in the Petition *{indicate paragraph number(s)}*: ___8, 9, 11; as to paragraph 15, I deny testing is required_____
_____.

3.   I currently am unable to admit or deny the allegations contained in the following paragraphs due to lack of information *{indicate paragraph number(s)}*: 12 and 13_____
_____.

4.   Since this case involves a minor child(ren), a completed Uniform Child Custody Jurisdiction and Enforcement Act Affidavit is filed with this Response.

5.   Child support should be determined in accordance with the worksheet form that ❑ is filed with this Response or ☒ will be filed after the other party serves his or her financial affidavit.

6.   A completed Financial Affidavit form ❑ is filed with this Response or ☒ will be timely filed after the other party serves his or her financial affidavit.

RESPECTFULLY SUBMITTED:

John Jones
_____
Signature of Respondent
Print Name: ___John Jones_____
Address: ___16 Northwood Street, #3___
___Happytown, Utopia___
Telephone: ___(555) 433-3333___

ACKNOWLEDGMENT

STATE OF __UTOPIA_____)
) SS.
COUNTY OF __BLISS_____)
I,____JOHN JONES_____, being first duly sworn upon my oath, depose and state that I am the Respondent in the above-entitled cause. I have read the attached RESPONSE TO PETITION TO ESTABLISH PATERNITY, CUSTODY AND TIME-SHARING, AND FOR CHILD SUPPORT. I state that the contents thereof are true and correct.

John Jones
_____
Signature of Respondent

SUBSCRIBED AND SWORN TO before me on
this __27th__ day of __August_____, __2006__.

Whit Ness
_____
NOTARY PUBLIC
My Commission Expires: ___October 23, 2008_____

IN THE CIRCUIT COURT
BLISS COUNTY, UTOPIA

SUSAN SMITH,   )
                Petitioner,   )
        v.   )   Case No. 06-12345
)
JOHN JONES,   )
                Respondent.   )

UNIFORM CHILD CUSTODY JURISDICTION
AND ENFORCEMENT ACT (UCCJEA) AFFIDAVIT

I, _____JOHN JONES_____{full legal name}, being sworn, certify that the following
statements are true:

1. The number of minor child(ren) subject to this proceeding is ___1___. The name, place of birth,
birth date, and sex of each child; the present address, periods of residence, and places where each
child has lived within the past five (5) years; and the name, present address, and relationship to the
child of each person with whom the child has lived during that time are:

THE FOLLOWING INFORMATION IS TRUE ABOUT CHILD # 1:

Child's Full Legal Name: _____Carrie Smith_____
Place of Birth: _Happytown, Utopia_   Date of Birth: _June 20, 2003_   Sex: _F_
Child's Residence for the past 5 years:

Dates (From/To)	Address (including city and state) where child lived	Name and present address of person child lived with	Relationship to child
Birth – present	222 Main Street, Happytown, Utopia	Petitioner Susan Smith, 222 Main Street, Happytown, Utopia	Mother
Birth – May, 2006	222 Main Street, Happytown, Utopia	Petitioner Susan Smith and Respondent John Jones	Mother & Father

2.   Participation in custody proceeding(s):
[check one only]

__XX__ I HAVE NOT participated as a party, witness, or in any capacity in any other litigation or custody proceeding in this or any other state, concerning custody of a child subject to this proceeding.

_____I HAVE participated as a party, witness, or in any capacity in any other litigation or custody proceeding in this or another state, concerning custody of a child subject to this proceeding.

Explain:
a. Name of each child: _____
b. Type of proceeding: _____
c. Court case number and state: _____
d. Date of court order or judgment (if any): _____

3.   Information about custody proceeding(s):
[check one only]

__XX__ I HAVE NO INFORMATION of any custody proceeding pending in a court of this or any other state concerning a child subject to this proceeding.
_____I HAVE THE FOLLOWING INFORMATION concerning a custody proceeding pending in a court of this or another state concerning a child subject to this proceeding, other than set out in item 2.

Explain:
a. Name of each child: _____
b. Type of proceeding: _____
c. Court case number and state: _____
d. Date of court order or judgment (if any): _____

4.   Persons not a party to this proceeding:
[check one only]

__XX__ I DO NOT KNOW OF ANY PERSON not a party to this proceeding who has physical custody or claims to have custody or visitation rights with respect to any child subject to this proceeding.
_____I KNOW THAT THE FOLLOWING NAMED PERSON(S) not a party to this proceeding has (have) physical custody or claim(s) to have custody or visitation rights with respect to any child subject to this proceeding:
a. Name and address of person:_____
    ( ) has physical custody ( ) claims custody rights ( ) claims visitation rights.
Name of each child: _____
b. Name and address of person: _____
    ( ) has physical custody ( ) claims custody rights ( ) claims visitation rights.
Name of each child: _____
c. Name and address of person: _____
    ( ) has physical custody ( ) claims custody rights ( ) claims visitation rights.
Name of each child:_____

5. Knowledge of prior child support proceedings:
[check one only]

XX The child(ren) described in this affidavit are NOT subject to existing child support order(s) in this or any state or territory.

____The child(ren) described in this affidavit are subject to the following existing child support order(s):

a. Name of each child: _____

b. Type of proceeding: _____

c. Court case number and state: _____

d. Date of court order or judgment (if any): _____

e. Amount of child support paid and by whom: _____

6.   I acknowledge that I have a continuing duty to advise this Court of any custody, visitation, child support, or guardianship proceeding (including dissolution of marriage,separate maintenance, child neglect, or dependency) concerning the child(ren) in this state or any other state about which information is obtained during this proceeding.

I certify that a copy of this document was [check one only]

 (X) mailed ( ) faxed and mailed ( ) hand delivered to the person(s) listed below on August 27, 2006 .
Other party or his/her attorney:
Name: Susan Smith
Address: 222 Main Street
City, State, Zip: Happytown, Utopia 11111
Fax Number:

I understand that I am swearing or affirming under oath to the truthfulness of the claims made in this affidavit and that the punishment for knowingly making a false statement includes fines and/or imprisonment.

Dated: August 27, 2006
Signature of Party   *John Jones*
Printed Name: John Jones
Address: 16 Northwood Street, #3
City, State, Zip: Happytown, Utopia 11111
Telephone Number: 555-433-3333
Fax Number:

STATE OF   Utopia
COUNTY OF Bliss

Sworn to or affirmed and signed before me on August 27, 2006
by   *Whit Ness*
NOTARY PUBLIC
 My Commission Expires: October 23, 2008

IN THE CIRCUIT COURT
BLISS COUNTY, UTOPIA

SUSAN SMITH,   )
           Petitioner,   )
   v.   )   Case No. 06-12345
)
JOHN JONES,   )
           Respondent.   )

CERTIFICATE OF SERVICE

I HEREBY CERTIFY that a copy of __Response to Petition to Establish Paternity, Custody__

__and Time-Sharing, and for Child Support; and Uniform Child Custody Jurisdiction and Enforcement__

__Act Affidavit__

_____ was:

      ☒ mailed   ❑ telefaxed and mailed   ❑ hand-delivered

to___Susan Smith, 222 Main Street, Happytown, Utopia_____

_____,

on ___August 27, 2006_____.

Dated: __August 27, 2006_____

                                John Jones
             _____
             Signature of ☒ Respondent or ❑ Petitioner
             Print Name: __John Jones_____
             Address: ___16 Northwood Street, #3_____
                     ___Happytown, Utopia_____
             Telephone: ___555-433-3333_____

IN THE CIRCUIT COURT
BLISS COUNTY, UTOPIA

SUSAN SMITH,   )
              Petitioner,   )
      v.   )   Case No. 06-12345
)
JOHN JONES,   )
              Respondent.   )

NOTICE OF HEARING

TO: [Enter Names and Addresses of the Parties/Attorneys to notify]

      John Jones
      1 Northwood Street, #3
      Happytown, Utopia

YOU ARE HEREBY NOTIFIED that the above cause is set for hearing as follows:

DATE: __September 25, 2006__   TIME: __9:30__   __A__ .m.

COURTHOUSE: __454 South Washington, Happytown, Utopia_____

JUDGE: __Barry D. Hatchett_____

SPECIFIC MATTER to be heard __Petitioner's Motion for Temporary Support and Custody__

NOTICED, DATED, AND MAILED this date: __August 31_____, __2006__

                          *Susan Smith*_____
                            Signature of party

IN THE CIRCUIT COURT
BLISS COUNTY, UTOPIA

SUSAN SMITH,	)	
Petitioner,	)	
v.	)	Case No. 06-12345
	)	
JOHN JONES,	)	
Respondent.	)	

MOTION FOR TEMPORARY RELIEF

NOW COMES _____Susan Smith_____, Petitioner, and states as follows:

1. That Petitioner filed her/~~his~~ Petition for ____Paternity, Custody and Time-Sharing,_____
   _____and for Child Support_____on ____July 15, 2006_____.

2. That Respondent filed a response to the petition on __August 27, 2006_____.

3. That _1_ child(~~ren~~) was/~~were~~ born to the parties, namely:

Name	Date of Birth	Age
Carrie Smith	June 20, 2003	3

who is/~~are~~ currently residing with Petitioner.

4. That Petitioner is presently ❏ unemployed ☒ employed and has a net income of approximately
   $__1,050.00_____ per month, and is without sufficient funds with which to support the minor
   child(~~ren~~).

5. That Petitioner has received no direct support from Respondent, except:
   for one $200 payment toward the minor child's birthday party, held on June 20, 2006.

6. That Respondent is presently gainfully employed and has a net income of approximately
   $_2,100___ per month, and has assets totaling in excess of $__14,000_____ and is well able
   to contribute to the support of the parties' minor child(~~ren~~); and Respondent has sufficient
   funds with which to pay for a just portion of the expenses of filing and maintaining this suit.

7. Attached to this Motion is the Petitioner's financial affidavit setting forth his/~~her~~ financial
   circumstances.

WHEREFORE, petitioner herein requests:

A. That Petitioner be granted temporary child support and temporary custody of the minor child(ren).

B. That Respondent be ordered to maintain existing comprehensive major medical and health care insurance coverage on the minor child(ren) and to pay the premiums on that insurance, and to provide Petitioner with a copy of the insurance policy.

C. That Respondent be ordered to pay a portion of the expenses of filing and maintaining this suit.

D. That Petitioner be granted such other and further relief as the court may deem just.

RESPECTFULLY SUBMITTED:

Susan Smith
_____
Signature of Petitioner
Print Name: _____ Susan Smith _____
Address: _____ 222 Main Street _____
_____ Happytown, Utopia _____
Telephone: _____ 555-444-4444 _____

ACKNOWLEDGMENT

STATE OF _____ UTOPIA _____)
) SS.
COUNTY OF _____ BLISS _____)

I, _____ Susan Smith _____, being first duly sworn upon my oath, depose and state that I am the Petitioner in the above-entitled cause. I have read the attached Motion. I state that the contents thereof are true and correct.

Susan Smith
_____
Signature of Petitioner

Subscribed and sworn to before me this
__31st__ day of _____ August _____, __2006__ .

C.U. Sine
_____
NOTARY PUBLIC
My Commission Expires: _____ May 5, 2008 _____

IN THE CIRCUIT COURT
BLISS COUNTY, UTOPIA

SUSAN SMITH,	)	
Petitioner,	)	
v.	)	Case No. 06-12345
	)	
JOHN JONES,	)	
Respondent.	)	

FINANCIAL AFFIDAVIT

THE AFFIANT, BEING DULY SWORN, SAYS UNDER PENALTY OF PERJURY THAT AFFIANT IS THE ☒ PETITIONER OR ❑ RESPONDENT IN THE ABOVE-CAPTIONED CASE, HAS PREPARED THIS FINANCIAL STATEMENT, KNOWS THE CONTENTS THEREOF, AND THAT IT IS TRUE AND CORRECT.

Name: __Susan Smith__   Date of Birth: __3-1-81__

I.   THE FOLLOWING INFORMATION IS TRUE ABOUT THE CHILDREN WHO ARE THE SUBJECT OF THIS PROCEEDING:

Names	Date of Birth	Person the child lives with
Carrie Smith	6-20-03	Susan Smith, 222 Main Street, Happytown, Utopia

II. PERSONAL INFORMATION

1.   Occupation: __Administrative Assistant__

2.   The highest year of education completed: __High School; currently a freshman at Happytown College__

3.   Are you presently employed? ☒ Yes ❑ No

a. If yes: (1) Where do you work (name and address)?

Gem Temporary Services

333 Main Street

Happytown, Utopia

(2) When did you start work there (month/year)?

9/04

b. If no: (1) When did you last work (month/year)?

(2) What were your gross monthly earnings? $_____

(3) Why are you presently unemployed?

III. INCOME INFORMATION

This information should be tailored and taken from the state's Child Support Worksheet(s).

4. MONTHLY GROSS/ NET INCOME. $1,166.00 /$1050.00

5. MISCELLANEOUS INCOME.

a. Child support received from other relationships $ -0-

b. Other miscellaneous income (list source and amounts) $ -0-

c. Total Miscellaneous Income (add lines 3.4a through 3.4c) $ -0-

6. Income of Other Adults in Household $ -0-

7. If the income of either party is disputed, state monthly income you believe is correct and explain below:

IV. AVAILABLE ASSETS

8. Cash on hand $ 50.00

9. On deposit in banks $ 249.00

10. Stocks and Bonds, cash value of life insurance $ -0-

11. Other liquid assets: $ -0-

V. MONTHLY EXPENSE INFORMATION

Monthly expenses for myself and __1__ dependent(s) are: (Expenses should be calculated for the future, after separation, based on the anticipated residential schedule for the children.)

12.   HOUSING.

Rent, 1st mortgage or contract payments	$ 325.00	
Installment payments for other mortgages		
or encumbrances	$ -0-	
Taxes & insurance (if not in monthly payment)	$ -0-	
Total Housing		$ 325

13.   UTILITIES.

Heat (gas & oil)	$ -0-	
Electricity	$ 24.00	
Water, sewer, garbage	$ -0-	
Telephone	$ 22.00	
Cable	$ 18.00	
Other	$ -0-	
Total Utilities		$ 64.00

14.   FOOD AND SUPPLIES.

Food for __2__ persons	$ 250.00	
Supplies (paper, tobacco, pets)	$ 100.00	
Meals eaten out	$ 40.00	
Other	$ -0-	
Total Food Supplies		$ 390.00

15.   CHILDREN.

Day Care/Babysitting	$ -0-	
Clothing	$ 125.00	
Tuition (if any)	$ -0-	
Other child related expenses	$ -0-	
Total Expenses Children		$ 125.00

16.   TRANSPORTATION.

Vehicle payments or leases	$ 49.00
Vehicle insurance & license	$ 30.00
Vehicle gas, oil, ordinary maintenance	$ 45.00
Parking	$ 15.00

Other transportation expenses $ -0-

Total Transportation $ 239.00

17. HEALTH CARE. (May be omitted if fully covered)

Insurance $ -0-

Uninsured dental, orthodontic, medical,
      and eye care expenses $ 40.00

Other uninsured health expenses $ -0-

Total Health Care $ 40.00

18. PERSONAL EXPENSES. (Not including children)

Clothing $ 65.00

Hair care/personal care expenses $ 25.00

Clubs and recreation $ -0-

Education $ 25.00

Books, newspapers, magazines, photos $ 25.00

Gifts $ 20.00

Other $ 40.00

Total Personal Expenses $ 192.50

19. MISCELLANEOUS EXPENSES.

Life insurance (if not deducted from income) $ 18.25

Other _____ $ -0-

Other _____ $ -0-

Total Miscellaneous Expenses $ 18.25

20. TOTAL HOUSEHOLD EXPENSES $ 1,394.25

VI. OTHER EXPENSES

21. INSTALLMENT DEBTS INCLUDED IN ABOVE PARAGRAPHS. (Include the creditor, balance, and last payment amount)

-0-

22. OTHER DEBTS AND MONTHLY EXPENSES NOT INCLUDED IN ABOVE PARAGRAPHS

-0-

Total Monthly Payments for Other Debts and Monthly Expenses $ -0-

23.   TOTAL EXPENSES $ 1,394.25

24.   Other: Cost of filing and expense of maintaining this suit:
          (clerk's fees, sheriff's service fees) $ 240.00

VII. SIGNATURE OF AFFIANT

Dated: ___August 31, 2006___   ___*Susan Smith*___

☒ Petitioner OR ❑ Respondent

SUBSCRIBED AND SWORN TO before me on
this __31st__ day of __August__, __2006__.

___*C.U. Sine*___

NOTARY PUBLIC

My Commission Expires: ___May 5, 2008___

IN THE CIRCUIT COURT
BLISS COUNTY, UTOPIA

SUSAN SMITH,   )
                    Petitioner,   )
        v.   )   Case No. ___06-12345___
)
JOHN JONES,   )
                    Respondent.   )

CHILD SUPPORT CALCULATION WORKSHEET

	Parent to Receive Supt	Parent to Pay Supt	Combined
1. Monthly gross income:	$ 1,166.00	$ 2,333.00	$ 3,499.00
2. Adjustments (per month):			
a. Other court or administratively ordered child support being paid:	($ -0-)	($ -0-)	
b. Court ordered spousal support being paid:	($ -0-)	($ -0-)	
c. Support obligation for children in primary physical custody:	($ -0-)	($ -0-)	
3. Adjusted monthly gross income (Line 1 minus lines 2a, 2b and 2c):	$ 1,166.00	$ 2,333.00	$ 3,499.00
4. Proportionate share of combined adjusted monthly gross income: (Each parent's line 3 divided by combined line 3):	33 %	66 %	
5. Basic child support amount (From support chart using combined line 3):			$ 636.00

	Parent to Receive Supt.	Parent to Pay Supt.	Combined
6. Additional child-rearing costs (per month):			
a. Reasonable work-related child care costs of the parent receiving support ($_____) less federal tax credit ($_____):	$ -0-		
b. Reasonable work-related child care costs of the parent paying support:		$ -0-	
c. Health insurance costs for children who are the subject of the proceeding:	$ -0-	$ -0-	
d. Uninsured extraordinary medical costs (Agreed by parents or ordered by court):	$ -0-	$ -0-	
e. Other extraordinary child-rearing costs (Agreed by parents or ordered by court):	$ -0-	$ -0-	
7. Total additional child rearing costs (Sum of lines 6a, 6b, 6c, 6d and 6e):	$ -0-	$ -0-	$ -0-
8. Total combined child support costs (Sum of lines 5 and combined 7):			$ 636.00

	Parent to Receive Supt.	Parent to Pay Supt.	Combined
9. Each parent's support obligation (Multiply line 8 by each parent's line 4):	$ 209.88	$ 419.76	
10. Credit for additional child-rearing costs of parent obligated to pay support:		($ -0-)	
11. Credit for a portion of the amounts expended by parent obligated to pay support during periods of temporary physical custody (Multiply line 5 by 20%):		($ 127.20)	
12. PRESUMED CHILD SUPPORT AMOUNT (Line 9 minus lines 10 and 11):	$ 292.56		

IN THE CIRCUIT COURT
BLISS COUNTY, UTOPIA

SUSAN SMITH,   )
                Petitioner,   )
        v.   )   Case No. 06-12345
)
JOHN JONES,   )
                Respondent.   )

ORDER FOR TEMPORARY RELIEF

This cause having come to be heard on _____September 25, 2006_____, upon Petitioner's Motion for Temporary Relief, it is HEREBY ORDERED:

1. That the Court has jurisdiction over the parties and subject matter of this action.

2. That Respondent shall pay child support in the amount of $__292.56__ per month, beginning ____October 1, 2006____.

3. That allocation of parenting time of the minor child(ren) be as follows:

    ☒ Petitioner ❑ Respondent shall be the primary residential parent, subject to parenting time in ❑ Petitioner ☒ Respondent as follows:
    every Tuesday 6-9 p.m.; alternating Thursdays, 6-9 p.m.; and alternating weekends from 5 p.m. Friday to 4 p.m. Sunday.

4. That ❑ Petitioner ☒ Respondent shall maintain existing comprehensive major medical and health care insurance coverage on the minor child(ren) and shall pay the premiums on that insurance, and shall provide ☒ Petitioner ❑ Respondent with a copy of the insurance policy.

5. That Respondent shall pay a just portion of the expenses of filing and maintaining this suit in the amount of $__160.00__.

ORDERED on __September 25, 2006__

_____Barry D. Hatchett_____
JUDGE

IN THE CIRCUIT COURT
BLISS COUNTY, UTOPIA

SUSAN SMITH,	)	
Petitioner,	)	
v.	)	Case No. 06-12345
	)	
JOHN JONES,	)	
Respondent.	)	

MOTION AND ORDER FOR REFERRAL TO MEDIATION

NOW COMES ___Susan Smith___, Petitioner, and states:

1.   That Petitioner filed a ___Petition to Establish Paternity, Custody and Time-Sharing, and___ ___for Child Support___ on ___July 15, 2006___.

2.   That Respondent filed a response to the petition on ___August 27, 2006___.

3.   That the following matter(s) is/are at issue in this case and is a/are proper subject(s) for mediation at this time:

☒ custody   ☒ time-sharing   ☒ child support   ☒ removal

WHEREFORE, Petitioner herein requests:

A.   That the matter(s) stated above be referred for mediation, and that a status date be set for 90 days to permit completion of the mediation sessions.

B.   That the costs of mediation be paid by ❑ petitioner ❑ respondent
       ☒ other: ___the parties in proportion to their incomes___

C.   That Petitioner be granted such other and further relief as the court may deem just.

Respectfully submitted,

Susan Smith
Signature of Petitioner
Print Name: ___Susan Smith___
Address: ___222 Main Street___
             ___Happytown, Utopia___
Telephone: ___555-444-4444___

ACKNOWLEDGMENT

STATE OF _____UTOPIA_____)
) SS.
COUNTY OF _____BLISS_____)

I,_____Susan Smith_____, being first duly sworn upon my oath, depose and state that I am the Petitioner in the above-entitled cause. I have read the attached MOTION FOR REFERRAL FOR MEDIATION. I state that the contents thereof are true and correct.

_____*Susan Smith*_____
Signature of Petitioner

SUBSCRIBED AND SWORN TO before me on
this __26th__ day of __September__, __2006__.

C. U. Sine
NOTARY PUBLIC
My Commission Expires: __May 5, 2008__

ORDER

This matter is hereby referred for mediation to: __Bliss County Circuit Court__
__Mediation Services__, as to the matters of:

☒ custody   ☒ time-sharing   ☒ child support   ☒ removal

A status date is set for __January 25, 2007__ to permit completion of the mediation sessions.

Costs of mediation shall be paid by: ❑ Petitioner ❑ Respondent

☒ other: __the parties in proportion to their incomes__

ORDERED ON __September 26, 2006__

Barry D. Hatchett
JUDGE

IN THE CIRCUIT COURT
BLISS COUNTY, UTOPIA

SUSAN SMITH,   )
          Petitioner,   )
    v.   )   Case No. 06-12345
)
JOHN JONES,   )
          Respondent.   )

PARENTING PLAN

1. Legal Custody

We agree to share joint legal custody of our child(xxx); that is, neither of us will make a major change affecting our child(xxx) in the areas of religion, residence, non-emergency medical care, education, or major recreational activities without consultation with the other. Before such a decision is made, we will discuss the matter and both of us must agree. If we cannot agree, our disagreement will be resolved by the methods we have chosen and set out in this parenting plan.

2. Time-Sharing

We will share time with the child(xxx) as follows:

Weekends and Weekdays (check one):

❑   Weekdays: _____

_____.

        Weekends: Weekends begin at _____ ___.m. (Friday) (Saturday) and end at _____ ___.m. (Sunday) (Monday), unless Monday is a legal holiday, in which case the weekend ends at _____ ___.m. (Monday) (Tuesday).

☒   We have attached a calendar for the year(s) ___2007 and 2008___ to this plan, and have marked in red the days the child(xxx) will spend with mother and in blue the days the child(xxx) will spend with father. Days for this calendar begin at _9:00 A_.m. and end at _6:00_ P.m.

Vacations (check one):

☒ Each parent will have uninterrupted time with the child(~~ren~~) for __2__ weeks each summer if that parent gives the other at least __30__ days notice.

❑ Until the youngest child reaches age ___, uninterrupted vacation time with a parent is limited to ___ weeks. Between the ages of ___ and ___, that time will be ___ weeks. Between the ages of ___ and ___, that time will be ___ weeks. After reaching age ___, vacation time will be ___ weeks.

Holidays: Regardless of the day of the week, the child(ren) will spend:

(a) Mother's Day and Mother's birthday with Mother;

(b) Father's Day and Father's birthday with Father;

(c) Child(~~ren~~)'s birthdays with ____Mother____ in even-numbered years and with ____Father____ in odd-numbered years.

(d) Child(~~ren~~) will spend holidays as follows:

	With Mother (Specify Year Odd/Even/Every)	With Father (Specify Year Odd/Even/Every)
New Year's Day	Odd	Even
Martin Luther King Day	Even	Odd
Presidents Day	Odd	Even
Memorial Day	Even	Odd
July 4th	Odd	Even
Labor Day	Even	Odd
Veterans Day	Odd	Even
Thanksgiving Day	Even	Odd
Christmas Eve	Odd	Even
Christmas Day	Even	Odd
Evening before Child's birthday	Even	Odd
Annual church picnic		Every
Annual mother-daughter church breakfast	Every	

Telephone: We agree that the child(ren) has/have a right to place phone calls to and receive phone calls from the absent parent.

Changes: Each of us is free to ask for exceptions to this schedule, but we understand that the other parent can say "no," and we will not argue about it.

Transportation: We will divide the responsibility for getting the child(ren) to and from each other's house, day care, school, etc., as follows:

Susan will drop Carrie at John's mother's house for John's parenting time. John will

be present or his mother may receive Carrie. John will return Carrie to Susan's mother's

house. Susan will be present or her mother may receive Carrie.

3. Trial Period or Permanent Plan: (Check one)

❏   We have not tried this time-sharing schedule before, so we agree that we will review the time-sharing plan in _____ days and at that time we will make any changes we agree on. If we cannot agree on changes, we will resolve our dispute using the method set forth in paragraph 6 below.

☒   We have already tried this time-sharing schedule, so we intend it to be permanent. We recognize, however, that as our child(ren) grow(s) and our lives change, it may be necessary to change the schedule from time to time. We agree that this is a major change that we have to discuss and agree on, and if necessary follow the dispute resolution procedures set out in paragraph 6 below.

4. The Status Quo—What we have now:

(a)   Doctor _____ Perry's Family Clinic, Happytown _____

(b)   Dentist _____ Doctor Tooth, Happytown _____

(c)   Other medical _ S. Bernard's Hospital _____

(d)   School _____ Marta Sterwart Elementary School _____

(e)   Religion _____ Catholic _____

(f)   Recreation _____ Happytown YMCA _____

We agree that neither of us will remove, cause to be removed, or permit removal of the child(ren) from the State of _____ Utopia _____, except for temporary visits which do not interfere with the time-sharing schedule, without the written consent of the other parent or resolution of the dispute by the method set forth in paragraph 6 below.

5. Emergencies

In case of a medical emergency, if time allows, the parent with that period of responsibility will contact the other parent concerning treatment of the child. If the absent parent cannot be reached, any decision for emergency medical treatment will be made in the best interest of the child by the available parent.

6. Dispute Resolution

We will discuss all major changes in the child(ren)'s lives in order to try to reach agreement. If we cannot agree after discussion, we will participate in counseling, conciliation, or mediation to try to reach agreement. We agree to share the cost of the mediator in proportion to our incomes. If there is still a dispute, we agree to submit the matter to the Court.

7. Review

We agree to review this Parenting Plan at least annually.

8. General Matters

In order to foster a continuing relationship between our child(ren) and both parents, we both agree:

(a)　To be actively involved in the major decisions and legal responsibilities of our child(ren).

(b)　To communicate and be flexible about the needs of our child(ren), especially as those needs change due to growth and development.

(c)　To be supportive of and positive about the child(ren)'s relationship with the other parent. Each of us will give loving permission to the child(ren) to enjoy the relationship with the other parent and neither of us will interfere with the parent-child relationship of the other.

(d)　That neither of us will align the child(ren) against the other parent or the other parent's family.

(e)　We agree that each of us is responsible to keep the other parent informed of the child(ren)'s school functions, parent-teacher conferences, and recreational activities.

I Agree:

Susan Smith
_____
Mother's Signature

I Agree:

John Jones
_____
Father's Signature

IN THE CIRCUIT COURT
BLISS COUNTY, UTOPIA

SUSAN SMITH,   )
          Petitioner,   )
      v.   )   Case No. 06-12345
)
JOHN JONES,   )
          Respondent.   )

REQUEST FOR HEARING

1. Type of case: _____Custody/Child Support_____

2. Judge to whom assigned: _____Barry D. Hatchett_____

3. Are there any hearings presently set? ___ Yes _X_ No

     If yes, when? _____

4. Specific matters to be heard [for example, petition for custody]:
    _____Agreement to Establish Custody and Time-Sharing, and for Support_____

5. Estimated total time required for hearing all parties and witnesses: _10 Minutes_____

6. Names, addresses, and phone numbers of all attorneys or parties to notify:

                         None

Hearing requested by: ____Agreement of Petitioner and Respondent_____
                    Petitioner/Respondent [circle one]

Date: ____January 25, 2007____

IN THE CIRCUIT COURT
BLISS COUNTY, UTOPIA

SUSAN SMITH,   )
        Petitioner,   )
   v.   )   Case No. 06-12345
)
JOHN JONES,   )
        Respondent.   )

FINAL JUDGMENT

THE COURT having read the pleadings, heard the evidence, and being otherwise advised, finds:

FINDINGS OF FACT

1.   Petitioner is a resident of _____Bliss_____ County, ____Utopia____ .

2.   Petitioner is the mother of the minor child(ren).

3.   Respondent is the father of the minor child(ren).

4.   The name(s), date(s) of birth, and age(s) of the minor child(ren) is/are

Name	Date of Birth	Age
Carrie Smith	June 20, 2003	3

WHEREFORE, THIS COURT ORDERS:

PATERNITY

1.   Respondent is hereby declared to be the natural father of the minor child(ren).

CUSTODY [Choose One]

❑ 2. Mother is awarded sole legal and physical custody of the minor child(ren) subject to the other parent's reasonable rights of visitation. Sole legal and physical custody is in the best interests of the minor child(ren) because:

☒ 2. Mother and Father are awarded joint legal custody of the minor child(ren), with primary physical custody in ☒ Mother ❑ Father, and periods of care and responsibility consistent with the best interests of the child(ren).

❑ 2. Custody is determined in accordance with the parenting plan attached to this judgment and by agreement of the parties.

CHILD SUPPORT [Check all that apply]

☒ 3. Child support is set according to the Child Support Guidelines and ❑ Mother ☒ Father is ordered to pay child support in the amount of $ 292.56 per month , beginning February 1, 2007 .

❑ 4. Child support in arrears are found to be $ _____ and ❑ Mother ❑ Father is ordered to pay child support arrears by paying an additional amount of $_____ per _____, beginning _____.

LIFE INSURANCE

☒ 5. ❑ Mother ☒ Father is ordered to purchase life insurance with a benefit amount of $ 15,000 , naming the ☒ Mother ❑ Father as trustee for the benefit of the minor child(ren) in order to pay the child support obligation upon the parent's death.

MEDICAL INSURANCE

☒ 6. ❑ Mother ☒ Father is ordered to provide health and dental insurance for the minor child(ren).

MEDICAL EXPENSES [Choose One]

❏   7.   ❏ Mother ❏ Father shall pay 100% of the child(ren)'s health and dental expenses not paid by insurance.

❏   7.   Mother and Father shall each pay one-half of the child(ren)'s health and dental expenses not paid by insurance.

☒   7.   Mother and Father shall pay the child(ren)'s health and dental expenses not paid by insurance in the percentages shown on the child support worksheet.

BIRTH RECORDS

❏   8.   The Department of Vital Statistics should be ordered to change the birth record of the minor child to reflect the paternity as determined by this court.

ENTERED: <u>January 22, 2007</u>

<u>Barry D. Hatchett</u>
Judge

AGREED: <u>Susan Smith</u>
           Petitioner

AGREED: <u>John Jones</u>
           Respondent

Blank Forms

The forms in this appendix will serve as guidelines for the more common forms you will need or encounter. They will undoubtedly need to be modified to fit the requirements and practices in the court where you will be filing your case. It is important that you understand the limitations of these forms and the importance of complying with the requirements of the courts in your area. If you have not already done so, be sure to read "Using Self-Help Law Books," beginning on page vii of this book.

Some states have standard forms that must be used in custody, visitation, and child support cases. If you are married, you will incorporate custody, visitation, and support requests (or agreements) into the divorce case (or legal separation or annulment).

Not all forms are used in every state (or county), and additional forms may be required. Check with your local court clerk to determine which legal forms are required and which are available through the clerk's office. If a form is required, but not available through your court clerk's office, adapt one of the forms from this book, following the formats for your state, or check your local law library for a state family law form book.

PROCEDURE

Most custody cases follow the same general procedure. A case is started by filing the original of a **PETITION TO ESTABLISH PATERNITY, CUSTODY AND TIME-SHARING, AND CHILD SUPPORT** (form 1) and **SUMMONS** (form 2) with the clerk of your court, and by serving copies of these papers on the other party. The party filing the **PETITION** is usually called the *petitioner* or *plaintiff*. The **PETITION** asks the court to establish paternity (if necessary), and award custody (or visitation) and child support to the petitioner. Many states also require that certain information be filed under the *Uniform Child Custody Jurisdiction and Enforcement Act*. In some states, this information is included in your **PETITION**; and in others, it will be on a separate form. A **RETURN OF SERVICE** (form 27) of the **PETITION** and **SUMMONS** on the respondent must be filed.

File the documents in the state in which you reside (or the child's state). Check with your clerk's office to determine the filing fee for filing the **PETITION**. If you cannot pay, check to determine how a court can waive or defer the fee.

The party responding to the **PETITION** is usually called the *respondent* or *defendant*. After being served the **SUMMONS** and **PETITION**, the respondent must file a written **RESPONSE TO PETITION** (form 3) with the clerk of the court within a certain number of days (usually twenty to thirty days depending on your state's laws, but may be longer if the respondent is served out of state). With that **RESPONSE** should be filed the relevant **UNIFORM CHILD CUSTODY JURISDICTION AND ENFORCEMENT ACT AFFIDAVIT** (form 4) (or *Uniform Child Custody Jurisdiction Act Affidavit*—check with your court clerk to see which form your state uses). Copies of the written response and affidavit must be sent to the petitioner (or the petitioner's lawyer), and **CERTIFICATE OF SERVICE** (form 5) must be filed with the clerk of the court.

To obtain records or the appearance of an individual, a **SUBPOENA** (form 17) may be sent. To obtain written answers under oath of the other party, **INTERROGATORIES** (form 18) may be sent. If paternity must be established (and this has not been requested in the **PETITION**), a **MOTION FOR SCIENTIFIC PATERNITY TESTING** (form 19) may be filed.

To properly establish child support, all states require some financial information disclosure from the parties, usually on specific forms that may be called **FINANCIAL AFFIDAVITS**, or *statements of financial means* or something similar (see form 8). Also, each state's child support guidelines are very specific, and nearly all states have adopted **CHILD SUPPORT CALCULATION WORKSHEET** forms (form 9) that must be filed prior to obtaining a child support order.

In addition, parties may file a **MOTION FOR TEMPORARY RELIEF** in court (such as temporary custody or support) (form 7) during the pendency of the case.

Either party may request the court to enter a child support order that deviates from the guideline amount. In some states, this is done by filling in a special section of the child support worksheet. In other states, a separate **MOTION TO DEVIATE FROM CHILD SUPPORT GUIDELINES** must be filed (form 21).

For parties who agree, a **PARENTING PLAN** (form 12 or form 13) should be filed with the court. (In some states, each party may file his or her own proposed parenting plan if there is no agreement.)

A **REQUEST FOR HEARING** of the **PETITION** or a **MOTION** and a **NOTICE OF HEARING** form (form 6) with a **CERTIFICATE OF SERVICE** upon the other party (form 5) may be sent as necessary to obtain a hearing on the petition or a motion filed.

If the respondent is served with the **PETITION** and **SUMMONS** but fails to file a written response within the required time period, the petitioner may file a **MOTION FOR DEFAULT** to request the court to enter an **ORDER OF DEFAULT** (forms 23 and 24) against the respondent with **CERTIFICATE OF SERVICE** (form 5) verifying that a copy was sent to the respondent.

Once the case is resolved a **FINAL JUDGMENT** (form 16) will be entered addressing custody/visitation and support (and paternity if necessary). If one of the parties disagrees with the trial court's decision, that party may appeal by filing a **NOTICE OF APPEAL** (form 25).

After the judgment is entered, if either party (or both) seeks to have the custody or support amount modified, and state law permits such a request, the party may file a **MOTION OF PETITION** or **MODIFY THE JUDGMENT** (form 26) and send (or serve) a copy to the other party (form 5, or forms 2 and 28).

Be sure to make extra copies of all the documents you file with the court and serve on the other parties, and keep a file-stamped copy for your records to prove you actually filed the document. Keep an organized file of all court papers, especially proof that you sent the documents to the other party, along with any letters concerning your case. This is important if a judge in your case needs to see a copy of a document that is not in your court file.

TABLE OF FORMS

FORM 1: PETITION TO ESTABLISH PATERNITY, CUSTODY
AND TIME-SHARING, AND FOR CHILD SUPPORT.............201

FORM 2: SUMMONS...206

FORM 3: RESPONSE TO PETITION TO ESTABLISH PATERNITY, CUSTODY
AND TIME-SHARING, AND FOR CHILD SUPPORT 207

FORM 4: UNIFORM CHILD CUSTODY JURISDICTION
AND ENFORCEMENT ACT (UCCJEA) AFFIDAVIT 209

FORM 5: CERTIFICATE OF SERVICE 213

FORM 6: NOTICE OF HEARING 214

FORM 7: MOTION FOR TEMPORARY RELIEF.........................215

FORM 8: FINANCIAL AFFIDAVIT 217

FORM 9: CHILD SUPPORT CALCULATION WORKSHEET...............222

FORM 10: ORDER FOR TEMPORARY RELIEF.........................225

FORM 11: MOTION AND ORDER FOR REFERRAL TO MEDIATION 226

FORM 12: PARENTING PLAN (ALTERNATIVE A)......................228

FORM 13: PARENTING PLAN (ALTERNATIVE B) 234

FORM 14: JOINT PARENTING AGREEMENT 238

FORM 15: REQUEST FOR HEARING................................241

FORM 16: FINAL JUDGMENT 242

FORM 17: SUBPOENA..245

FORM 18: INTERROGATORIES....................................246

FORM 19: MOTION FOR SCIENTIFIC PATERNITY TESTING 250

FORM 20: ORDER FOR SCIENTIFIC PATERNITY TESTING 251

FORM 21: MOTION TO DEVIATE FROM CHILD SUPPORT GUIDELINES 253

FORM 22: ORDER PERMITTING DEVIATION
FROM CHILD SUPPORT GUIDELINES 258

FORM 23: MOTION FOR DEFAULT 259

FORM 24: ORDER OF DEFAULT 260

FORM 25: NOTICE OF APPEAL 261

FORM 26: PETITION TO MODIFY JUDGMENT OF CUSTODY
AND/OR CHILD SUPPORT 262

FORM 27: ORDER MODIFYING JUDGMENT 266

FORM 28: RETURN OF SERVICE 268

PETITION TO ESTABLISH PATERNITY, CUSTODY AND TIME-SHARING, AND FOR CHILD SUPPORT

NOW COMES _____, Petitioner, and states as follows:

1.   Petitioner is a resident of _____ County.

2.   _____ is the mother of the minor child(ren).

3.   _____ is the father of the minor child(ren).

4.   The name, date of birth, and age of the minor child(ren) is/are:
      <u>Name</u>   <u>Date of Birth</u>   <u>Age</u>

PATERNITY [Choose 1]

❑   5.   Paternity has not been established.
❑   5.   Paternity has been established by:
      ❑   Respondent has acknowledged his paternity of the minor child(ren) in writing filed with the Department of Vital Statistics in the State in which the child(ren) was/were born.
      ❑   Respondent has consented to paternity and is named as father on the minor child(ren)'s birth certificate.
      ❑   Paternity of the minor child(ren) has been established by blood tests.
      ❑   Respondent has openly held out the minor child(ren) as his natural child(ren) and established a personal, financial, or custodial relationship with the child(ren).

HOME STATE AND RESIDENCE OF CHILDREN
6. A completed declaration under the Uniform Child Custody Jurisdiction And Enforcement Act Affidavit is attached to this petition.

7. The number of minor child(ren) subject to this proceeding is _____. The name, place of birth, birth date, and sex of each child; the present address, periods of residence, and places where each child has lived within the past five (5) years; and the name, present address, and relationship to the child of each person with whom the child has lived during that time are:

THE FOLLOWING INFORMATION IS TRUE ABOUT CHILD # 1:

Child's Full Legal Name: _____
Place of Birth: _____Date of Birth: _____Sex: _____
Child's Residence for the past 5 years:

Dates (From/To)	Address (including city and state) where child lived	Name and present address of person child lived with	Relationship to child

THE FOLLOWING INFORMATION IS TRUE ABOUT CHILD # 2:

Child's Full Legal Name: _____
Place of Birth: _____Date of Birth: _____Sex: _____
Child's Residence for the past 5 years:

Dates (From/To)	Address (including city and state) where child lived	Name and present address of person child lived with	Relationship to child

CUSTODY OPTIONS [Choose 1]

❑ 8. The parties should be awarded joint legal custody of the minor child(ren), with primary physical custody in and periods of care and responsibility consistent with the best interests of the child(ren).

❑ 8. Petitioner should be awarded sole legal and physical custody of the child(ren) subject to the respondent's reasonable rights of visitation. Sole legal and physical custody is in the best interests of the minor child(ren) because:

CHILD SUPPORT

❑ 9. Child support should be set according to this state's support guidelines and the Respondent should be ordered to pay child support in the amount determined by the child support guidelines. A worksheet form and financial affidavit will be timely filed and served on Respondent.

❑ 10. Petitioner requests temporary child support during the pendency of this case, in accordance with this state's child support guidelines.

❑ 11. Petitioner requests that child support be retroactive to the birth of the child(ren), and that the amount of child support be in accordance with this state's child support guidelines.

LIFE INSURANCE

❑ 12. Respondent should be ordered to purchase life insurance with a benefit amount of $_____, naming the petitioner as trustee for the benefit of the minor child(ren) to pay the child support obligation upon the respondent's death.

MEDICAL INSURANCE

❑ 13. _____ should provide health and dental insurance for the minor child(ren).

MEDICAL EXPENSES [Choose 1]

❑ 14. _____ should pay 100% of the minor child(ren)'s health and dental expenses not paid by insurance.

❑ 14. The parties should each pay one-half of the child(ren)'s health and dental expenses not paid by insurance.

❑ 14. The parties should pay the child(ren)'s health and dental expenses not paid by insurance in the income percentages shown on the child support worksheet.

SCIENTIFIC TESTING

❑ 15. Petitioner requests scientific paternity testing be ordered if Respondent denies paternity of the child(ren), with blood or other bodily tissue or fluid samples to be sent for testing to a qualified blood testing laboratory and DNA tests, HLA tests, and any other tests the testing facility recommends to be performed. Petitioner requests that court costs, scientific testing costs, and expert witness fees should be ordered to be paid by Respondent.

BIRTH RECORD

❑ 16. Upon determination of paternity, the Department of Vital Statistics should be ordered to change the birth record of the minor child(ren) to reflect the paternity as determined by this court.

WHEREFORE, Petitioner asks the Court to:

1. Establish the paternity of the minor child(ren).
2. Award child custody in accordance with this Petition.
3. Order child support according to the Child Support Guidelines.
4. Grant such other and further relief as the Court deems just and equitable.

RESPECTFULLY SUBMITTED:

_____
Signature of Petitioner
Print Name: _____
Address: _____
_____
Telephone: _____

ACKNOWLEDGMENT

STATE OF _____)

) SS.

COUNTY OF _____)

I,_____, being first duly sworn upon my oath, depose and state that I am the Petitioner in the above-entitled cause. I have read the attached PETITION TO ESTABLISH PATERNITY, CUSTODY AND TIME-SHARING, AND FOR CHILD SUPPORT. I state that the contents thereof are true and correct, except to the matters stated on information and belief, and those matters I believe to be true.

_____

Signature of Petitioner

SUBSCRIBED AND SWORN TO before me on
this _____ day of _____, _____.

_____

NOTARY PUBLIC
My Commission Expires: _____

SUMMONS

TO THE RESPONDENT:
    Name of Respondent: _____
    Address: _____

To the Officer: This summons must be served by the Officer or other person to whom it was given for service, with the endorsement of service within 30 days after its date.

To the respondent: You are summoned and required to file an answer to the complaint in this case, a copy of which is attached to this summons. You must answer or otherwise respond within ____ days after service of this summons. If you fail to do so, a judgment of default may be entered against you for the relief requested in the complaint.

ISSUED this _____ day of _____, _____

                    _____
                    Clerk of the District Court
                    By _____

RESPONSE TO PETITION TO ESTABLISH PATERNITY, CUSTODY AND TIME-SHARING, AND FOR CHILD SUPPORT

I, _____, the Respondent, herein certify that the following information is true:

1.   I admit the allegations contained in the following numbered paragraphs in the Petition *{indicate paragraph number(s)}*: _____
_____.

2.   I deny the allegations contained in the following numbered paragraphs in the Petition *{indicate paragraph number(s)}*: _____
_____.

3.   I currently am unable to admit or deny the allegations contained in the following paragraphs due to lack of information *{indicate paragraph number(s)}*: _____
_____.

4.   Since this case involves a minor child(ren), a completed Uniform Child Custody Jurisdiction and Enforcement Act Affidavit is filed with this Response.

5.   Child support should be determined in accordance with the worksheet form which ❑ is filed with this Response or ❑ will be filed after the other party serves his or her financial affidavit.

6.   A completed Financial Affidavit form ❑ is filed with this Response or ❑ will be timely filed after the other party serves his or her financial affidavit.

RESPECTFULLY SUBMITTED:

_____
Signature of Respondent
Print Name: _____
Address: _____
            _____
Telephone: _____

ACKNOWLEDGMENT

STATE OF _____)

) SS.

COUNTY OF _____)

I,_____, being first duly sworn upon my oath, depose and state that I am the Respondent in the above-entitled cause. I have read the attached RESPONSE TO PETITION TO ESTABLISH PATERNITY, CUSTODY AND TIME-SHARING, AND FOR CHILD SUPPORT. I state that the contents thereof are true and correct.

_____

Signature of Respondent

SUBSCRIBED AND SWORN TO before me on
this _____ day of _____, _____.

_____

NOTARY PUBLIC
My Commission Expires: _____

UNIFORM CHILD CUSTODY JURISDICTION
AND ENFORCEMENT ACT (UCCJEA) AFFIDAVIT

I, _____{full legal name}, being sworn, certify that the following statements are true:

1. The number of minor child(ren) subject to this proceeding is _____. The name, place of birth, birth date, and sex of each child; the present address, periods of residence, and places where each child has lived within the past five (5) years; and the name, present address, and relationship to the child of each person with whom the child has lived during that time are:

THE FOLLOWING INFORMATION IS TRUE ABOUT CHILD # 1:

Child's Full Legal Name: _____
Place of Birth: _____Date of Birth: _____Sex: _____
Child's Residence for the past 5 years:

Dates (From/To)	Address (including city and state) where child lived	Name and present address of person child lived with	Relationship to child/present*

THE FOLLOWING INFORMATION IS TRUE ABOUT CHILD # 2:

Child's Full Legal Name: _____

Place of Birth: _____Date of Birth: _____Sex: _____

Child's Residence for the past 5 years:

Dates (From/To)	Address (including city and state) where child lived	Name and present address of person child lived with	Relationship to child/present*

2.   Participation in custody proceeding(s):
[check one only]

____I HAVE NOT participated as a party, witness, or in any capacity in any other litigation or custody proceeding in this or any other state, concerning custody of a child subject to this proceeding.
____I HAVE participated as a party, witness, or in any capacity in any other litigation or custody proceeding in this or another state, concerning custody of a child subject to this proceeding.

Explain:
a. Name of each child: _____
b. Type of proceeding: _____
c. Court case number and state: _____
d. Date of court order or judgment (if any): _____

3.   Information about custody proceeding(s):
[check one only]

_____I HAVE NO INFORMATION of any custody proceeding pending in a court of this or any other state concerning a child subject to this proceeding.
_____I HAVE THE FOLLOWING INFORMATION concerning a custody proceeding pending in a court of this or another state concerning a child subject to this proceeding, other than set out in item 2.

Explain:
a. Name of each child: _____
b. Type of proceeding: _____
c. Court case number and state: _____
d. Date of court order or judgment (if any): _____

4.   Persons not a party to this proceeding:
[check one only]

_____I DO NOT KNOW OF ANY PERSON not a party to this proceeding who has physical custody or claims to have custody or visitation rights with respect to any child subject to this proceeding.
_____I KNOW THAT THE FOLLOWING NAMED PERSON(S) not a party to this proceeding has (have) physical custody or claim(s) to have custody or visitation rights with respect to any child subject to this proceeding:
a. Name and address of person: _____
    ( ) has physical custody ( ) claims custody rights ( ) claims visitation rights.
Name of each child: _____
b. Name and address of person: _____
    ( ) has physical custody ( ) claims custody rights ( ) claims visitation rights.
Name of each child: _____
c. Name and address of person: _____
    ( ) has physical custody ( ) claims custody rights ( ) claims visitation rights.
Name of each child: _____

5. Knowledge of prior child support proceedings:
[check one only]

_____The child(ren) described in this affidavit are NOT subject to existing child support order(s) in this or any state or territory.
_____The child(ren) described in this affidavit are subject to the following existing child support order(s):
a. Name of each child: _____
b. Type of proceeding: _____
c. Court case number and state: _____
d. Date of court order or judgment (if any): _____
e. Amount of child support paid and by whom: _____

6.   I acknowledge that I have a continuing duty to advise this Court of any custody, visitation, child support, or guardianship proceeding (including dissolution of marriage,separate maintenance, child neglect, or dependency) concerning the child(ren) in this state or any other state about which information is obtained during this proceeding.

I certify that a copy of this document was [check one only]
( ) mailed ( ) faxed and mailed ( )
hand delivered to the person(s) listed below on {date}
.

Other party or his/her attorney:
Name: _____
Address: _____
City, State, Zip: _____
Fax Number: _____

I understand that I am swearing or affirming under oath to the truthfulness of the claims made in this affidavit and that the punishment for knowingly making a false statement includes fines and/or imprisonment.

Dated: _____
Signature of Party _____
Printed Name: _____
Address: _____
City, State, Zip: _____
Telephone Number: _____
Fax Number: _____

STATE OF _____
COUNTY OF _____

Sworn to or affirmed and signed before me on   August 27, 2006
by _____
NOTARY PUBLIC

CERTIFICATE OF SERVICE

I HEREBY CERTIFY that a copy of _____

_____

_____

_____ *{name of document(s) served}* was:

    ❑ mailed   ❑ telefaxed and mailed   ❑ hand-delivered

to_____

_____

{name and address of person being served}, on _____ *{date}*.

Dated: _____

                _____

                Signature of ❑ Respondent or ❑ Petitioner

                Print Name: _____

                Address: _____

                                 _____

                Telephone: _____

NOTICE OF HEARING

TO: [Enter Names and Addresses of the Parties/Attorneys to notify]

YOU ARE HEREBY NOTIFIED that the above cause is set for hearing as follows:

DATE: _____   TIME: _____ ____.m.

COURTHOUSE: _____

JUDGE: _____

SPECIFIC MATTER to be heard _____

NOTICED, DATED, AND MAILED this date: _____, _____

_____
Signature of party

MOTION FOR TEMPORARY RELIEF

NOW COMES _____, Petitioner, and states as follows:

1.   That Petitioner filed her/his Petition for _____

_____on _____.

2.   That Respondent filed a response to the petition on _____.

3.   That ____ child(ren) was/were born to the parties, namely:
      Name   Date of Birth   Age

who is/are currently residing with Petitioner.

4.   That Petitioner is presently ❏ unemployed ❏ employed and has a net income of approximately $_____ per month, and is without sufficient funds with which to support the minor child(ren).

5.   That Petitioner has received no direct support from Respondent, except:

6.   That Respondent is presently gainfully employed and has a net income of approximately $_____ per month, and has assets totaling in excess of $_____ and is well able to contribute to the support of the parties' minor child(ren); and Respondent has sufficient funds with which to pay for a just portion of the expenses of filing and maintaining this suit.

7.   Attached to this Motion is the Petitioner's financial affidavit setting forth his/her financial circumstances.

WHEREFORE, Petitioner herein requests:

A. That Petitioner be granted temporary child support and temporary custody of the minor child(ren).

B. That Respondent be ordered to maintain existing comprehensive major medical and health care insurance coverage on the minor child(ren) and to pay the premiums on that insurance, and to provide Petitioner with a copy of the insurance policy.

C. That Respondent be ordered to pay a portion of the expenses of filing and maintaining this suit.

D. That Petitioner be granted such other and further relief as the court may deem just.

RESPECTFULLY SUBMITTED:

_____

Signature of Petitioner
Print Name: _____
Address: _____
                    _____
Telephone: _____

ACKNOWLEDGMENT

STATE OF _____)
) SS.
COUNTY OF _____)

I, _____, being first duly sworn upon my oath, depose and state that I am the Petitioner in the above-entitled cause. I have read the attached Motion. I state that the contents thereof are true and correct.

_____

Signature of Petitioner

Subscribed and sworn to before me this
_____ day of _____, _____.

_____
NOTARY PUBLIC
My Commission Expires: _____

FINANCIAL AFFIDAVIT

THE AFFIANT, BEING DULY SWORN, SAYS UNDER PENALTY OF PERJURY THAT AFFIANT IS THE ❑ PETITIONER OR ❑ RESPONDENT IN THE ABOVE-CAPTIONED CASE, HAS PREPARED THIS FINANCIAL STATEMENT, KNOWS THE CONTENTS THEREOF, AND THAT IT IS TRUE AND CORRECT.

Name: _____ Date of Birth: _____

I. THE FOLLOWING INFORMATION IS TRUE ABOUT THE CHILDREN WHO ARE THE SUBJECT OF THIS PROCEEDING:

Names	Date of Birth	Person Child Lives With

II. PERSONAL INFORMATION

1.   Occupation: _____

2.   The highest year of education completed: _____

3.   Are you presently employed? ❑ Yes ❑ No

    a. If yes: (1)   Where do you work (name and address)?

                                       _____

                                       _____

                                       _____

            (2)   When did you start work there (month/year)?

                                         _____

b. If no: (1) When did you last work (month/year)?

_____

(2) What were your gross monthly earnings? $_____

(3) Why are you presently unemployed?

_____

III. INCOME INFORMATION

This information should be tailored and taken from the state's Child Support Worksheet(s).

4. MONTHLY GROSS/ NET INCOME. $_____/$_____

5. MISCELLANEOUS INCOME.
    a. Child support received from other relationships $_____
    b. Other miscellaneous income (list source and amounts) $_____
    c. Total Miscellaneous Income (add lines 3.4a through 3.4c) $_____

6. Income of other adults in household $_____

7. If the income of either party is disputed, state monthly income you believe is correct and explain below:

IV. AVAILABLE ASSETS

8. Cash on hand $_____

9. On deposit in banks $_____

10. Stocks and bonds, cash value of life insurance $_____

11. Other liquid assets: $_____

V. MONTHLY EXPENSE INFORMATION

Monthly expenses for myself and _____ dependent(s) are: (Expenses should be calculated for the future, after separation, based on the anticipated residential schedule for the children.)

12. HOUSING.
Rent, first mortgage or contract payments $_____
Installment payments for other mortgages
        or encumbrances $_____
Taxes & insurance (if not in monthly payment) $_____
        Total Housing $_____

13. UTILITIES.
      Heat (gas & oil) $_____
      Electricity $_____
      Water, sewer, garbage $_____
      Telephone $_____
      Cable $_____
      Other $_____
      Total Utilities $_____

14. FOOD AND SUPPLIES.
      Food for _____ persons $_____
      Supplies (paper, tobacco, pets) $_____
      Meals eaten out $_____
      Other $_____
      Total Food Supplies $_____

15. CHILDREN.
      Day Care/Babysitting $_____
      Clothing $_____
      Tuition (if any) $_____
      Other child related expenses $_____
      Total Expenses Children $_____

16. TRANSPORTATION.
      Vehicle payments or leases $_____
      Vehicle insurance & license $_____
      Vehicle gas, oil, ordinary maintenance $_____
      Parking $_____
      Other transportation expenses $_____
      Total Transportation $_____

17. HEALTH CARE. (May be omitted if fully covered)
      Insurance $_____
      Uninsured dental, orthodontic, medical,
            and eye care expenses $_____
      Other uninsured health expenses $_____
      Total Health Care $_____

18.   PERSONAL EXPENSES (Not including children).
Clothing $_____
Hair care/personal care expenses $_____
Clubs and recreation $_____
Education $_____
Books, newspapers, magazines, photos $_____
Gifts $_____
Other $_____
Total Personal Expenses $_____

19.   MISCELLANEOUS EXPENSES.
Life insurance (if not deducted from income) $_____
Other _____ $_____
Other _____ $_____
Total Miscellaneous Expenses $_____

20.   TOTAL HOUSEHOLD EXPENSES $_____

VI. OTHER EXPENSES

21.   INSTALLMENT DEBTS INCLUDED IN ABOVE PARAGRAPHS. (Include the creditor, balance and last payment amount)

22.   OTHER DEBTS AND MONTHLY EXPENSES NOT INCLUDED IN ABOVE PARAGRAPHS

Total Monthly Payments for Other Debts and Monthly Expenses $_____

23.   TOTAL EXPENSES $_____

24.   Other: Cost of filing and expense of maintaining this suit:
      (clerk's fees, sheriff's service fees) $_____

VII. SIGNATURE OF AFFIANT

Dated: _____

_____
❏ Petitioner OR ❏ Respondent

SUBSCRIBED AND SWORN TO before me on
this _____ day of _____, _____.

_____
NOTARY PUBLIC
My Commission Expires: _____

CHILD SUPPORT CALCULATION WORKSHEET

	Parent to Receive Supt.	Parent to Pay Supt.	Combined
1. Monthly gross income:	$_____	$_____	$_____
2. Adjustments (per month):			
a. Other court or administratively ordered child support being paid:	($_____)	($_____)	
b. Court ordered spousal support being paid:	($_____)	($_____)	
c. Support obligation for children in primary physical custody:	($_____)	($_____)	
3. Adjusted monthly gross income (Line 1 minus lines 2a, 2b and 2c):	$_____	$_____	$_____
4. Proportionate share of combined adjusted monthly gross income: (Each parent's line 3 divided by combined line 3):	____%	____%	
5. Basic child support amount (from support chart using combined line 3):			$_____

	Parent to Receive Supt.	Parent to Pay Supt.	Combined
6. Additional child-rearing costs (per month):			
a. Reasonable work-related child care costs of the parent receiving support ($_____) less federal tax credit ($_____):	$_____		
b. Reasonable work-related child care costs of the parent paying support:		$_____	
c. Health insurance costs for children who are the subject of the proceeding:	$_____	$_____	
d. Uninsured extraordinary medical costs (Agreed by parents or ordered by court):	$_____	$_____	
e. Other extraordinary child-rearing costs (Agreed by parents or ordered by court):	$_____	$_____	
7. Total additional child rearing costs (Sum of lines 6a, 6b, 6c, 6d and 6e):	$_____	$_____	$_____
8. Total combined child support costs (Sum of lines 5 and combined 7):			$_____

	Parent to Receive Supt.	Parent to Pay Supt.	Combined
9. Each parent's support obligation (Multiply line 8 by each parent's line 4):	$_____	$_____	
10. Credit for additional child-rearing costs of parent obligated to pay support:		($_____)	
11. Credit for a portion of the amounts expended by parent obligated to pay support during periods of temporary physical custody (Multiply line 5 by 20%):		($_____)	
12. PRESUMED CHILD SUPPORT AMOUNT (Line 9 minus lines 10 and 11):	$_____		

ORDER FOR TEMPORARY RELIEF

This cause having come to be heard on _____, upon Petitioner's Motion for Temporary Relief, it is HEREBY ORDERED:

1. That the court has jurisdiction over the parties and subject matter of this action.

2. That Respondent shall pay child support in the amount of $_____ per month, beginning _____.

3. That allocation of parenting time of the minor child(ren) be as follows:

    ❏ Petitioner ❏ Respondent shall be the primary residential parent, subject to parenting time in ❏ Petitioner ❏ Respondent as follows:

4. That ❏ Petitioner ❏ Respondent shall maintain existing comprehensive major medical and health care insurance coverage on the minor child(ren) and shall pay the premiums on that insurance, and shall provide ❏ Petitioner ❏ Respondent with a copy of the insurance policy.

5. That Respondent shall pay a just portion of the expenses of filing and maintaining this suit in the amount of $_____.

ORDERED on _____

_____
JUDGE

MOTION AND ORDER FOR REFERRAL TO MEDIATION

NOW COMES _____, Petitioner, and states:

1. That Petitioner filed a _____
   on _____.

2. That Respondent filed a response to the petition on _____.

3. That the following matter(s) is/are at issue in this case and is/are proper subject(s) for mediation at this time:

   ❏ custody   ❏ time-sharing   ❏ child support   ❏ removal

WHEREFORE, petitioner herein requests:

A. That the matter(s) stated above be referred for mediation, and that a status date be set for 90 days to permit completion of the mediation sessions.

B. That the costs of mediation be paid by   ❏ Petitioner ❏ Respondent
   ❏ other:_____

C. That Petitioner be granted such other and further relief as the court may deem just.

Respectfully submitted,

_____
Signature of Petitioner
Print Name: _____
Address: _____
             _____
Telephone: _____

ACKNOWLEDGMENT

STATE OF _____)

) SS.

COUNTY OF _____)

I,_____, being first duly sworn upon my oath, depose and state that I am the Petitioner in the above-entitled cause. I have read the attached MOTION FOR REFERRAL FOR MEDIATION. I state that the contents thereof are true and correct.

_____

Signature of Petitioner

SUBSCRIBED AND SWORN TO before me on this _____ day of _____, _____.

_____

NOTARY PUBLIC

My Commission Expires: _____

ORDER

This matter is hereby referred for mediation to: _____ _____, as to the matters of:

❏ custody   ❏ time-sharing   ❏ child support   ❏ removal

A status date is set for _____ to permit completion of the mediation sessions.

Costs of mediation shall be paid by: ❏ Petitioner   ❏ Respondent

❏ other: _____

ORDERED ON _____

_____

JUDGE

PARENTING PLAN

I.   GENERAL INFORMATION

This parenting plan applies to the following children:

<u>Name</u>   <u>Birth Date</u>

II.   RESIDENTIAL SCHEDULE

These provisions set forth where the child(ren) shall reside each day of the year and what contact the child(ren) shall have with each parent.

A.   PRESCHOOL SCHEDULE

❑ There are no children of preschool age.
❑ Prior to enrollment in school, the child(ren) shall reside with the

❑ mother   ❑ father, except for the following days and times when the child(ren) will reside with or be with the other parent:

from: _____[day and time]
to: _____[day and time]

❑ every week   ❑ every   other week   ❑ the first and third week of the month
❑ the second and fourth week of the month   ❑ other:

from: _____[day and time]
to: _____[day and time]

❑ every week ❑ every other week ❑ the first and third week of the month
❑ the second and fourth week of the month ❑ other:

B.   SCHOOL SCHEDULE

Upon enrollment in school, the child(ren) shall reside with the ❑ mother ❑ father, except for the following days and times when the child(ren) will reside with or be with the other parent:

from: _____[day and time]
to: _____[day and time]

❑ every week ❑ every other week ❑ the first and third week of the month
❑ the second and fourth week of the month ❑ other:

from: _____[day and time]
to: _____[day and time]

❑ every week ❑ every other week ❑ the first and third week of the month
❑ the second and fourth week of the month ❑ other:

❑ The school schedule will start when each child begins
❑ kindergarten ❑ first grade ❑ other: _____

C.   SCHEDULE FOR WINTER VACATION

The child(ren) shall reside with the ❑ mother ❑ father during winter vacation, except for the following days and times when the child(ren) will reside with or be with the other parent:

D.   SCHEDULE FOR SPRING VACATION

The child(ren) shall reside with the ❑ mother ❑ father during spring vacation, except for the following days and times when the child(ren) will reside with or be with the other parent:

E.   SUMMER SCHEDULE

Upon completion of the school year, the child(ren) shall reside with the ❑ mother ❑ father, except for the following days and times when the child(ren) will reside with or be with the other parent:

❑ Same as school year schedule.
❑ Other:

F.   VACATION

❏ Does not apply.
❏ The schedule for vacation with parents is as follows:

G.   SCHEDULE FOR HOLIDAYS

The residential schedule for the child(ren) for the holidays listed below is as follows:

	With Mother (Specify Year Odd/Even/Every)	With Father (Specify Year Odd/Even/Every)
New Year's Day	_____	_____
Martin Luther King Day	_____	_____
Presidents' Day	_____	_____
Memorial Day	_____	_____
July 4th	_____	_____
Labor Day	_____	_____
Veterans Day	_____	_____
Thanksgiving Day	_____	_____
Christmas Eve	_____	_____
Christmas Day	_____	_____
_____	_____	_____
_____	_____	_____
_____	_____	_____
_____	_____	_____

❏ For purposes of this parenting plan, a holiday shall begin and end as follows (set forth times):
❏ Holidays which fall on a Friday or a Monday shall include Saturday and Sunday.
❏ Other:

H.   SCHEDULE FOR SPECIAL OCCASIONS

The residential schedule for the child(ren) for the following special occasions (i.e., birthdays) is as follows:

Occasion	With Mother (Specify Year Odd/Even/Every)	With Father (Specify Year Odd/Even/Every)

❏ Other:

I.   PRIORITIES UNDER THE RESIDENTIAL SCHEDULE

❏ Does not apply.
❏ For purposes of this parenting plan the following days shall have priority:
❏ Parents' vacations have priority over holidays. Holidays have priority over other special occasions. Special occasions have priority over school vacations.
❏ Other:

J.   TRANSPORTATION ARRANGEMENTS

Transportation arrangements for the child(ren), other than costs, between parents shall be as follows:

K.   DESIGNATION OF CUSTODIAN

The children named in this parenting plan are scheduled to reside the majority of the time with the ❏ mother ❏ father. This parent is designated the custodian of the child(ren) solely for purposes of all other state and federal statutes which require a designation or determination of custody. This designation shall not affect either parent's rights and responsibilities under this parenting plan.

III.   DECISION MAKING

A.   DAY-TO-DAY DECISIONS

Each parent shall make decisions regarding the day-to-day care and control of each child while the child is residing with that parent. Regardless of the allocation of decision making in this parenting plan, either parent may make emergency decisions affecting the health or safety of the children.

B.   MAJOR DECISIONS

Major decisions regarding each child shall be made as follows:

Education decisions	❏ Mother	❏ Father	❏ joint
Nonemergency health care	❏ Mother	❏ Father	❏ joint
Religious upbringing	❏ Mother	❏ Father	❏ joint
	❏ Mother	❏ Father	❏ joint
	❏ Mother	❏ Father	❏ joint
	❏ Mother	❏ Father	❏ joint
	❏ Mother	❏ Father	❏ joint
	❏ Mother	❏ Father	❏ joint
	❏ Mother	❏ Father	❏ joint

IV. DISPUTE RESOLUTION

Disputes between the parties, other than child support disputes, shall be submitted to (list person or agency):

❏ counseling by _____
❏ mediation by _____
❏ arbitration by _____

The cost of this process shall be allocated between the parties as follows:

❏ _____% Mother   _____❏ Father.
❏ based on each party's proportional share of income from the child support worksheets.
❏ as determined in the dispute resolution process.

The counseling, mediation, or arbitration process shall be commenced by notifying the other party by ❏ written request ❏ certified mail ❏ other:

In the dispute resolution process:

(a)   Preference shall be given to carrying out this Parenting Plan.

(b)   Unless an emergency exists, the parents shall use the designated process to resolve disputes relating to implementation of the plan, except those related to financial support.

(c)   A written record shall be prepared of any agreement reached in counseling or mediation and of each arbitration award and shall be provided to each party.

(d)   If the court finds that a parent has used or frustrated the dispute resolution process without good reason, the court shall award attorneys' fees and financial sanctions to the other parent.

(e)   The parties have the right of review from the dispute resolution process to the superior court.

V. OTHER PROVISIONS

❏ There are no other provisions.
❏ There are the following other provisions:

VI. SIGNATURES FOR PARENTING PLAN

_____

Mother
Date and Place of Signature

_____

Father
Date and Place of Signature

PARENTING PLAN

1. Legal Custody

We agree to share joint legal custody of our child(ren); that is, neither of us will make a major change affecting our child(ren) in the areas of religion, residence, nonemergency medical care, education or major recreational activities without consultation with the other. Before such a decision is made, we will discuss the matter and both of us must agree. If we cannot agree, our disagreement will be resolved by the methods we have chosen and set out in this parenting plan.

2. Time-Sharing

We will share time with the child(ren) as follows:

Weekends and Weekdays (check one):

❑   Weekdays: _____

_____.

Weekends: Weekends begin at _____ ___.m. (Friday) (Saturday) and end at _____ ___.m. (Sunday) (Monday), unless Monday is a legal holiday, in which case the weekend ends at _____ ___.m. (Monday) (Tuesday).

❑   We have attached a calendar for the year(s) _____ to this plan, and have marked in red the days the child(ren) will spend with Mother and in blue the days the child(ren) will spend with Father. Days for this calendar begin at _____ ___.m. and end at _____ ___.m.

Vacations (check one):

❑   Each parent will have uninterrupted time with the child(ren) for _____ weeks each summer if that parent gives the other at least _____ days notice.

❑   Until the youngest child reaches age ___, uninterrupted vacation time with a parent is limited to ___ weeks. Between the ages of ___ and ___, that time will be ___ weeks. Between the ages of ___ and ___, that time will be ___ weeks. After reaching age ___, vacation time will be ___ weeks.

Holidays: Regardless of the day of the week, the child(ren) will spend:

(a)   Mother's Day and Mother's birthday with mother;

(b)   Father's Day and Father's birthday with Father;

(c)   Child(ren)'s birthdays with _____ in even-numbered years and with _____ in odd-numbered years.

(d)   Child(ren) will spend holidays as follows:

	With Mother (Specify Year Odd/Even/Every)	With Father (Specify Year Odd/Even/Every)
New Year's Day	_____	_____
Martin Luther King Day	_____	_____
Presidents' Day	_____	_____
Memorial Day	_____	_____
July 4th	_____	_____
Labor Day	_____	_____
Veterans Day	_____	_____
Thanksgiving Day	_____	_____
Christmas Eve	_____	_____
Christmas Day	_____	_____
_____	_____	_____
_____	_____	_____
_____	_____	_____
_____	_____	_____
_____	_____	_____

Telephone: We agree that the child(ren) has/have a right to place phone calls to and receive phone calls from the absent parent.

Changes: Each of us is free to ask for exceptions to this schedule, but we understand that the other parent can say "no," and we will not argue about it.

Transportation: We will divide the responsibility for getting the child(ren) to and from each other's house, day care, school, etc., as follows:

_____

_____

_____

_____

_____.

3. Trial Period or Permanent Plan: (Check one)

❑ We have not tried this time-sharing schedule before, so we agree that we will review the time-sharing plan in ____ days and at that time we will make any changes we agree on. If we cannot agree on changes, we will resolve our dispute using the method set forth in paragraph 6 below.

❑ We have already tried this time-sharing schedule, so we intend it to be permanent. We recognize, however, that as our child(ren) grow(s) and our lives change, it may be necessary to change the schedule from time to time. We agree that this is a major change that we have to discuss and agree on, and if necessary follow the dispute resolution procedures set out in paragraph 6 below.

4. The Status Quo—What we have now:

(a) Doctor _____

(b) Dentist _____

(c) Other medical _____

(d) School _____

(e) Religion _____

(f) Recreation _____

We agree that neither of us will remove, cause to be removed, or permit removal of the child(ren) from the State of _____, except for temporary visits which do not interfere with the time-sharing schedule, without the written consent of the other parent or resolution of the dispute by the method set forth in paragraph 6 below.

5. Emergencies

In case of a medical emergency, if time allows, the parent with that period of responsibility will contact the other parent concerning treatment of the child. If the absent parent cannot be reached, any decision for emergency medical treatment will be made in the best interest of the child by the available parent.

6. Dispute Resolution

We will discuss all major changes in the child(ren)'s lives in order to try to reach agreement. If we cannot agree after discussion, we will participate in counseling, conciliation, or mediation to try to reach agreement. If there is still a dispute, we agree to submit the matter to the court.

7. General Matters

In order to foster a continuing relationship between our child(ren) and both parents, we both agree:

(a)   To be actively involved in the major decisions and legal responsibilities of our child(ren).

(b)   To communicate and be flexible about the needs of our child(ren), especially as those needs change due to growth and development.

(c)   To be supportive of and positive about the child(ren)'s relationship with the other parent. Each of us will give loving permission to the child(ren) to enjoy the relationship with the other parent and neither of us will interfere with the parent-child relationship of the other.

(d)   That neither of us will align the child(ren) against the other parent or the other parent's family.

(e)   We agree that each of us is responsible to keep the other parent informed of the child(ren)'s school functions, parent-teacher conferences, and recreational activities.

I Agree: I Agree:

_____   _____

Mother's Signature   Father's Signature

JOINT PARENTING AGREEMENT

This is the agreement of _____ and _____, the parents of the minor child(ren) listed below. We agree that we will serve as joint custodians of our children and will jointly determine all major decisions including those related to education, school, religion, medical care, and all other questions related to the health and welfare of our children.

I. Child Information
     Names   Date of Birth

II. Statement of Agreement
We recognize that both parents are fit and proper persons to have joint custody of our children. We possess the ability to cooperate effectively with the best interests of our children as our guiding principle in this agreement. There are no issues of abuse that exist between the parties.

Each parent agrees to promptly share with the other any school related information, including parent/teacher conferences, school meeting and programs, athletic schedules and any other activities in which the children are involved.

Each parent agrees to promptly notify the other if he or she is unable to keep a planned visit or parenting obligation with the children.

Each parent will keep the other informed as to his/her address, phone number and employer information.

Each parent shall have reasonable telephone and Internet access to the children.

III. Residence

A. _____ (children) shall live primarily with _____ (parent) who shall have the daily responsibility to make medical and educational decisions concerning the children.

B. _____ [*nonresidential parent*] shall have parenting time (or visitation) with the children as follows:
[check all that apply]

1. ____ Every _____ from ____ a.m./p.m. to ____ a.m./p.m.
2. ____ Every weekend or _____ alternating weekends as follows:
    __ Friday ____ from ____ a.m./p.m. to Saturday ____ a.m./p.m.
    __ Friday ____ from ____ a.m./p.m. to Sunday ____ a.m./p.m.
    __ Saturday____ from ____ a.m./p.m. to Saturday ____ a.m./p.m.
    __ Saturday ____ from ____ a.m./p.m. to Sunday ____ a.m./p.m.
    __ Sunday ____ from ____ a.m./p.m. to Sunday ____ a.m./p.m.

3. Major holidays as follows:

Major Holidays	Even Number Years	Odd Number Years

4. School vacations including summer, spring and winter breaks as follows:

5. Other:

C. Transportation
Parents shall provide for transportation as follows:

IV. Emergency Care

A. In a medical emergency, the parent who is with the child or the first parent to make contact with the child shall make all necessary medical decisions and promptly notify the other parent.

B. Each parent will notify the other of any serious medical illness or injury and must provide the other with any medication for the children.

V. Removal

We each agree that neither will remove the children permanently from the state except by agreement or as permitted by a court if based on the best interests of the children.

VI. Mediation

If we cannot agree on any vital decision affecting the health, education or welfare of our children, we agree that any dispute should be referred for mediation prior to applying to a court for relief. We agree to share the cost of the mediator in proportion to our incomes. If mediation fails or we cannot agree on a mediator, then a court proceeding may be filed by either parent.

VII. Review

We agree to review this Joint Parenting Agreement at least annually.

_____   _____
Petitioner   Respondent

_____ date   _____ date

REQUEST FOR HEARING

1. Type of case: _____

2. Judge to whom assigned: _____

3. Are there any hearings presently set? ___ Yes ___ No

    If yes, when? _____

4. Specific matters to be heard [for example, petition for custody]:

5. Estimated total time required for hearing all parties and witnesses: _____

6. Names, addresses, and phone numbers of all attorneys or parties to notify:

Hearing requested by: _____
                            Petitioner/Respondent [circle one]

Date: _____

FINAL JUDGMENT

THE COURT having read the pleadings, heard the evidence, and being otherwise advised, finds:

FINDINGS OF FACT

    1.   The Petitioner is a resident of _____ County, _____.

    2.   Petitioner is the mother of the minor child(ren).

    3.   Respondent is the father of the minor child(ren).

    4.   The name(s), date(s) of birth, and age(s) of the minor child(ren) is/are:

<u>Name</u>   <u>Date of Birth</u>   <u>Age</u>

WHEREFORE, THIS COURT ORDERS:

PATERNITY

    1.   Respondent is hereby declared to be the natural father of the minor child(ren).

CUSTODY [Choose One]

❑   2.   Mother is awarded sole legal and physical custody of the minor child(ren) subject to the other parent's reasonable rights of visitation. Sole legal and physical custody is in the best interests of the minor child(ren) because:

❑ 2.   Mother and Father are awarded joint legal custody of the minor child(ren), with primary physical custody in ❑ Mother ❑ Father, and periods of care and responsibility consistent with the best interests of the child(ren).

❑ 2.   Custody is determined in accordance with the parenting plan attached to this judgment and by agreement of the parties.

CHILD SUPPORT [Check all that apply]

❑ 3.   Child support is set according to the Child Support Guidelines and ❑ Mother ❑ Father is ordered to pay child support in the amount of $_____ per _____, beginning _____.

❑ 4.   Child support in arrears is found to be $ _____ and ❑ Mother ❑ Father is ordered to pay child support arrears by paying an additional amount of $_____ per _____, beginning _____.

LIFE INSURANCE

❑ 5.   ❑ Mother ❑ Father is ordered to purchase life insurance with a benefit amount of $_____, naming ❑ Mother ❑ Father as trustee for the benefit of the minor child(ren) in order to pay the child support obligation upon the parent's death.

MEDICAL INSURANCE

❑ 6.   ❑ Mother ❑ Father is ordered to provide health and dental insurance for the minor child(ren).

MEDICAL EXPENSES [Choose One]

❑ 7.   ❑ Mother ❑ Father shall pay 100% of the child(ren)'s health and dental expenses not paid by insurance.

❑ 7.   Mother and Father shall each pay one-half of the child(ren)'s health and dental expenses not paid by insurance.

❑ 7.   Mother and Father shall pay the child(ren)'s health and dental expenses not paid by insurance in the percentages shown on the child support worksheet.

BIRTH RECORDS

❏   8.   The Department of Vital Statistics should be ordered to change the birth record of the minor child to reflect the paternity as determined by this court.

_____   _____
Judge   Date

AGREED: _____
               Petitioner

AGREED: _____
               Respondent

SUBPOENA

TO:

YOU ARE HEREBY COMMANDED to appear before the Honorable _____
_____, Judge of the above-entitled court, on
_____ {date}, at _____ {time}, in Courtroom _____, at
the _____ Courthouse located
at: _____

YOU ARE COMMANDED ALSO to bring the following:

**YOUR FAILURE TO APPEAR IN RESPONSE TO THIS SUBPOENA WILL SUBJECT YOU
TO PUNISHMENT FOR CONTEMPT OF THIS COURT.**

ISSUED this _____ day of _____, _____
                                                  Clerk of the Court

                          By _____

PARTY REQUESTING SUBPOENA:

Name: _____
Address: _____
_____
Telephone No.: _____

INTERROGATORIES

TO:

You are hereby requested to answer the following under oath within _____ days of the date of the service hereof:

1.   State your full name, current address, date of birth, and Social Security number.

2.   List your education by school, date, and degree.

3.   State the number, age, and relationship of all persons presently residing with you.

4.   List all employment held by you during the preceding three years. With regard to each employment, state the name and address of each employer; your position, job title, or job description; if you had an employment contract; the date on which you commenced your employment and, if applicable, the date and reason for the termination of your employment; your current gross and net income per pay period; your gross income and social security wages as shown on the last W-2 tax and wage statement received by you, and the deductions shown thereon; and all additional benefits received from your employment stating the type and value thereof.

5.   During the preceding three years, have you had any source of income other than from your employment listed above? If so, with regard to each source of income, state the following: the source of income, including the type of income and the name and address of the source; the frequency with which you receive income from the source; the amount of income received by you from the source during the immediately preceding three years; and the amount of income received by you from the source for each month during the immediately preceding three years.

6.   State your monthly expenses for the previous 12 months, including living, personal, entertainment, stating to whom and the amount paid.

7. State the name, address, and phone number of all mental and physical health care providers you and/or your child(ren) have seen in the past three years, including the date and nature of service and the amount paid.

8. Do you own any life, annuity, or endowment insurance policies? If so, with regard to each such policy, state: the name, address, and phone number of the company; the policy number; the face value of the policy; the present value of the policy; the amount of any loan or encumbrance on the policy; the date of acquisition of the policy; and the beneficiary or beneficiaries.

9. Do you have any right, title, claim, or interest in or to a pension plan, retirement plan, or profit sharing plan, including, but not limited to, individual retirement accounts (IRAs), 401(k) plans, and deferred compensation plans? If so, with regard to each such plan or account, state: the name and address of the entity providing the plan; the date of your initial participation in the plan; and the amount of funds currently held on your behalf under the plan.

10. State the name and address of any accountant, tax preparer, bookkeeper, and other person, firm, or entity who has kept or prepared books, documents, and records with regard to your income, property, business, or financial affairs during the past three years.

11. State the name and address of each witness who will testify at trial, and state the subject of each witness' testimony.

12. List every document you intend to produce at trial.

13. State the name and address of each expert or opinion witness who will offer any testimony, and state: the subject matter on which the witness is expected to testify; the conclusions and/or opinions of the witness and the basis therefore, including reports of the witness, if any; the qualifications of each opinion witness, including a curriculum vitae and/or resumé, if any; and the identity of any written reports of the witness regarding an issue in this suit.

14. Has/have the child(ren) made statements to you that reveal attitudes toward custody/visitation? If so, state the contents of the statements, to whom made, and date made.

15. State all acts committed, and words spoken, by the other parent which adversely affected the child(ren) by dates, nature, persons present, and how it affected the child(ren).

16. If you had primary care of the child(ren), what are your goals and plans for the next twenty-four months? State the name, address, and phone number of persons who would be involved in the daily care of the child(ren).

17. To what extent do you contribute to the care of the people with whom you live, and his/her child support?

18. Specify all vacations, or other trips taken with the person you live with since _____ (date) by nature, date, and source of funds.

19. List all sums you spend on the person you live with and his/her child(ren) for Christmas, holidays, and birthdays since _____ (date).

20. Have you used an illegal or controlled substance in the past three years? If so, state type, amount, and duration of use by date.

21. Why do you believe it is in the child(ren)'s best interest for you to be custodian/joint custodian of the child(ren), and why would it not be in the child(ren)'s best interests for the other parent to be?

To the person answering: Furnish all information available to you. Answer every portion you can, and provide an explanation of your efforts if you cannot answer. These interrogatories are continuing and you must supplement your answers as necessary. You are reminded that your answers are under oath and subject to penalties for perjury.

_____
Signature of Sending Party

CERTIFICATE OF SERVICE

A true and accurate copy of this notice and attachments was ❑ hand-delivered or

❑ faxed to _____ or ❑ placed in the United States mail, postage prepaid, to the above party on the following date: _____.

Dated: _____   _____

Signature of ❑ Petitioner ❑ Respondent

SUBSCRIBED AND SWORN TO before me this _____ day of _____, _____.

_____

NOTARY PUBLIC
My Commission Expires: _____.

Attestation
(for answering party)

STATE OF   )

) SS.

COUNTY OF   )

_____, being first duly sworn on oath, deposes and states that he/she is a ❏ petitioner ❏ respondent in the above-captioned matter, that he/she has read the foregoing document, and the answers made herein are true, correct, and complete to the best of his/her knowledge and belief.

_____
Signature

SUBSCRIBED AND SWORN TO before me this

_____ day of _____, _____.

_____

NOTARY PUBLIC
My Commission Expires: _____.

MOTION FOR SCIENTIFIC PATERNITY TESTING

❏ Petitioner ❏ Respondent certifies that the following information is true:

1.   At this time, other than testimony, very little or no substantial proof of paternity or nonpaternity is available in this action.

2.   I request that the Court enter an order for appropriate scientific testing of the biological samples of Petitioner and Respondent, and the minor child(ren) listed below, so that a determination of paternity of the minor child(ren) can be made to a reasonable degree of medical certainty:

    Name   Birth date

3.   I request that the costs of the scientific testing initially be borne by:

    ❏ Petitioner ❏ Respondent ❏ both Petitioner and Respondent.

Dated: _____

_____
Signature of Party

Printed Name: _____

Address: _____

City, State, Zip: _____

Telephone Number: _____

Fax Number: _____

ORDER FOR SCIENTIFIC PATERNITY TESTING

This cause having come to be heard on _____, on the Motion for Scientific Paternity Testing, and the court being fully advised in the premises,

IT IS HEREBY ORDERED:

1.   That the above motion is GRANTED.

2.   That the Petitioner, Respondent, and the minor child(ren) shall appear for the purpose of appropriate scientific testing: [Select one only]

❑ a. Immediately

❑ b. at _____ a.m./p.m., on _____, at _____ _____.

❑ c. at a time and place to be specified by _____ _____. Appropriate scientific testing on Petitioner, Respondent, and the minor child(ren) shall be at _____ _____, with at least 30 days advance written notice.

3.   The costs of the scientific paternity testing shall be assessed:

❑ at a later date   ❑ against Petitioner   ❑ against Respondent

❑ Other {explain} _____

4.   The test results, opinions, and conclusions of the test laboratory shall be filed with the Court. Any objection to the test results must be made in writing and must be filed with the Court at least ten days before the hearing. If no objection is filed, the test results shall be admitted into evidence. Nothing in this paragraph prohibits a party from calling an outside expert witness to refute or support the testing procedure or results, or the mathematical theory on which they are based.

5.   Test results are admissible in evidence and should be weighed along with other evidence of the paternity of the alleged father unless the statistical probability of paternity equals or exceeds 95%. A statistical probability of 95% or more creates a rebuttable presumption that the alleged father is the biological father of the child(ren). If the party fails to rebut the presumption of paternity, the Court may enter a summary judgment of paternity. If the test results show the alleged father cannot be the biological father, the case shall be dismissed with prejudice.

6.   The Court reserves jurisdiction over the parties and the subject matter of this action to enforce the terms and provisions of this and all previous orders as well as to enter such other orders as may be just.

ORDERED ON _____

_____

JUDGE

MOTION TO DEVIATE FROM CHILD SUPPORT GUIDELINES

❏ Petitioner or ❏ Respondent requests that the Court enter an order granting the following:

SECTION I

[✔ one only (a or b)]

❏ a. MORE child support than the amount required by the child support guidelines. The Court should order MORE child support than the amount required by the child support guidelines because of:

[✔ all that apply to your situation]

❏   1.   Extraordinary medical, psychological, educational, or dental expenses.

❏   2.   Seasonal variations in one or both parent's income.

❏   3.   Age(s) of the child(ren), taking into consideration the greater needs of older child(ren).

❏   4.   Special needs that have been met traditionally within the family budget even though the fulfilling of those needs will cause support to exceed the guidelines.

❏   5.   Refusal of the nonresidential parent to become involved in the activities of the child(ren).

❏   6.   Due consideration given to the primary residential parent's homemaking services.

❏   7.   Total available assets of mother, father, and child(ren).

❏   8.   Impact of IRS dependency exemption and waiver of that exemption.

❑ 9. Residency of subsequently born or adopted child(ren) with the obligor, including consideration of the subsequent spouse's income.

❑ 10. Any other adjustment that is needed to achieve an equitable result, which may include reasonable and necessary expenses jointly incurred during the marriage.

Explain any items marked above:

❑ b. LESS child support than the amount required by the child support guidelines. The Court should order LESS child support than the amount required by the child support guidelines because of:

[✔ all that apply to your situation]

❑ 1. Extraordinary medical, psychological, educational, or dental expenses.

❑ 2. Independent income of child(ren), excluding the child(ren)'s SSI income.

❑ 3. Payment of both child support and spousal support to a parent that regularly has been paid and for which there is a demonstrated need.

❑ 4. Seasonal variations in one or both parent's income.

❑ 5. Age of the child(ren), taking into consideration the greater needs of older child(ren).

❑ 6. The child(ren) spend(s) a substantial amount of time with the nonresidential parent, thereby reducing expenses of the primary residential parent.

❑ 7. Due consideration given to the primary residential parent's homemaking services.

❑ 8. Visitation with nonresidential parent for more than twenty-eight consecutive days.

❑ 9. Total available assets of obligee, obligor, and child(ren).

❑ 10. Impact of IRS dependency exemption and waiver of that exemption.

❑ 11. Application of the child support guidelines requires the obligor to pay more than 55% of gross income for a single support order.

❑ 12. Any other adjustment that is needed to achieve an equitable result, which may include reasonable and necessary expenses jointly incurred during the marriage.

Explain any items marked above:

SECTION II. INCOME AND ASSETS OF CHILD(REN) COMMON TO BOTH PARTIES

List the total of any independent income or assets of the child(ren) common to both parties (income from Social Security, gifts, stocks/bonds, employment, trust fund(s), investment(s), etc.). Attach an explanation.

TOTAL VALUE OF ASSETS OF CHILD(REN) $_____

TOTAL MONTHLY INCOME OF CHILD(REN) $_____

SECTION III. EXPENSES FOR CHILD(REN) COMMON TO BOTH PARTIES

1. Monthly babysitting, or other child care $_____

2. Monthly after-school care $_____

3. Monthly school tuition $_____

4. Monthly school supplies, books, and fees $_____

5. Monthly after-school activities $_____

6. Monthly lunch money $_____

7. Monthly private lessons/tutoring $_____

8. Monthly allowance $_____

9. Monthly clothing $_____

10. Monthly uniforms $_____

11. Monthly entertainment (movies, birthday parties, etc.) $_____

12. Monthly health and dental insurance premiums $_____

13. Monthly medical, dental, prescription charges (unreimbursed) $_____

14. Monthly psychiatric/psychological/counselor (unreimbursed) $_____

15. Monthly orthodontic (unreimbursed) $_____

6. Monthly grooming $_____

17. Monthly nonprescription medications/cosmetics/toiletries/sundries $_____

18. Monthly gifts from children to others (other children,

    relatives, teachers, etc.) $_____

19. Monthly camp or other summer activities $_____

20. Monthly clubs (Boy/Girl Scouts, etc.) or recreational fees $_____

21. Monthly visitation expenses (for nonresidential parent) $_____

    Explain:

22. Monthly insurance (life, etc.) {explain}: $_____

Other {explain}:

23. _____ $_____

24. _____ $_____

25. _____ $_____

26. TOTAL EXPENSES FOR CHILD(REN) COMMON TO

BOTH PARTIES (add lines 1 through 25) $_____

_____

Signature of Party

Printed Name: _____

Address: _____

City, State, Zip: _____

Telephone Number: _____

Fax Number: _____

ORDER PERMITTING DEVIATION FROM CHILD SUPPORT GUIDELINES

THE COURT, having reviewed the Motion for Deviation from Child Support Guidelines, any response which may have been filed, and otherwise being fully advised in the premises, HEREBY ORDERS:

1.   Based on the calculations derived from the child support guidelines, the presumed amount of child support under the guidelines is $_____.

2.   Deviation from the child support guidelines is appropriate because:

3.   The ❑ Petitioner ❑ Respondent is ordered to pay child support in the amount of $_____ per month, beginning on _____.

ORDERED ON _____

_____

JUDGE

MOTION FOR DEFAULT

Petitioner hereby requests this court to enter a default against the respondent for failure to respond to the petition filed on _____ and served upon Respondent on _____.

RESPECTFULLY SUBMITTED:

_____

Signature of Petitioner

Print Name: _____

Address: _____

Telephone: _____

ORDER OF DEFAULT

A default is hereby entered against the Respondent, _____, for failure to serve or file a response in this action as required by law.

DATED: _____

_____

NOTICE OF APPEAL

TO: [Enter Names and Addresses of the parties/attorneys to notify]

YOU ARE HEREBY NOTIFIED that on _____[date], I have filed the within NOTICE of APPEAL against a judgment entered on: _____.

NOTICED DATED AND MAILED this date: _____

_____
Signature of party

PETITION TO MODIFY JUDGMENT OF CUSTODY AND/OR CHILD SUPPORT

The ❏ Petitioner ❏ Respondent, _____, states as follows:

1.   On _____, _____, Judge _____ entered a judgment for custody with a parenting plan. A certified copy of the custody decree/parenting plan to be modified is filed with or attached to this petition, if the decree or plan to be modified was entered in another county or state.

2.   The custody judgment/parenting plan should be modified because a substantial change of circumstances has occurred in the circumstances of the children or the other party and the modification is in the best interests of the children and is necessary to serve the best interests of the children. This request is based on the factors below.

    ❏   The parents agree to the modification.

    ❏   The children have been integrated into my family with the consent of the other parent in substantial deviation from the prior decree or parenting plan.

    ❏   The children's present environment is detrimental to the children's physical, mental, or emotional health and the harm likely to be caused by a change in environment is outweighed by the advantage of a change to the children.

    ❏   The requested modification or adjustment of the prior custody decree/parenting plan is based upon the following substantial change in circumstance:

3. The most recent support order was entered in _____
_____{county and state} on _____ {date}. The order
requires _____ {name} to pay $_____ per month for the sup-
port of {list name(s) of the child(ren)}:

4. The order of child support should be modified for the following reasons.
    ❑   The previous order was entered more than ___ years ago and there has been a change
        in the income of the parents.
    ❑   _____ {name of child} is in need of postsecondary edu-
        cational support because the child is in fact dependent and is relying upon the parents
        for the reasonable necessities of life.
    ❑   _____ {name of child} is a dependent adult child and
        support should be extended beyond his or her eighteenth birthday.
    ❑   The previous order was entered by default.
    ❑   The previous order was entered more than a year ago and:
        ❑   The order works a severe economic hardship.
        ❑   The child has moved to a new age category for support purposes.
        ❑   The child is still in high school and there is a need to extend support beyond
            the child's eighteenth birthday to allow the child to complete high school.
        ❑   Either or both parents should be required to maintain or provide health
            insurance coverage.
    ❑   There has been the following substantial change of circumstances since the order was
        entered (explain):

WHEREFORE, ❏ PETITIONER OR ❏ RESPONDENT hereby requests this court to:

1.   Enter an order establishing child support in conjunction with the proposed parenting plan, the child support worksheet, and financial declaration which have been filed with this petition.

2.   Adopt a temporary parenting plan until further hearing in this matter.

3.   Other:

    ❏   Ordering child support payments which are based upon the State Child Support Schedule. A copy of the child support worksheet is filed with this action.

    ❏   Requiring a periodic adjustment of support.

    ❏   Extending child support beyond _____'s *{name of child}* eighteenth birthday to allow the child to complete high school.

    ❏   Extending child support beyond _____'s *{name of child}* eighteenth birthday until he/she is no longer dependent upon either or both parents and is capable of self-support.

    ❏   Allowing for postsecondary educational support for _____ _____ *{name of child}*.

    ❏   Ordering the payment of day care.

    ❏   Ordering the payment of educational expenses.

    ❏   Ordering the payment of long distance transportation expenses.

    ❏   Ordering the payment of uncovered health care expenses.

    ❏   Awarding the tax exemption for the children as follows:

Dated: _____   _____

                     Signature

_____

Print or Type Name

ACKNOWLEDGMENT

STATE OF _____)
)
) ss
)
COUNTY OF _____)

I, _____, being first duly sworn upon my oath, depose and state that I am Petitioner in the above-entitled cause. I have read the attached **PETITION TO MODIFY JUDGMENT OF CUSTODY AND CHILD SUPPORT**. I state that the contents thereof are true and correct, except to the matters stated on information and belief, and those matters I believe to be true.

_____
Signature of Party

SUBSCRIBED AND SWORN TO before me on

this _____ day of _____, _____.

_____
NOTARY PUBLIC

My Commission Expires: _____

ORDER MODIFYING JUDGMENT

THE COURT FINDS:

1.   This case has come before this Court on a petition to modify the_____
_____, dated _____, regarding
the matter(s) of:

    ❑ Child custody   ❑ Visitation   ❑ Child support.

2.   This court has jurisdiction to modify the judgment and over the parties.

3.   This Order applies to the following child(ren):

<u>Name</u>   <u>Birth Date</u>   <u>Age</u>

4.   Grounds for Changing Custody/Parenting Plan:

❑ The parents agree to the modification.

❑ The requisite time period has passed and there has been a substantial change in circumstances that make a change in custody/visitation in the best interest of the child(ren) for
the reasons described below:

❑ There has been domestic violence, spousal abuse, or child abuse as described below since the date of the earlier order, and it is in the best interest of the child(ren) that the change is made for the reasons described below:

❑ The child(ren)'s current environment may seriously endanger the child(ren)'s physical, mental, moral, or emotional health, the child(ren) is/are at risk under the current order, and it is in the best interest of the child(ren) that custody is changed for the reasons described below:

5.   Grounds for Changing Child Support:

❑ The parents agree to the change

❑ The requisite time period has passed and there has been a change in circumstances that make changing child support justified for the reasons described below:

WHEREFORE, THE COURT ORDERS that the _____ _____, dated _____, is amended as follows:

ORDERED _____

_____

JUDGE

RETURN OF SERVICE

I, being duly sworn, on oath, say that I am over the age of eighteen (18) years and not a party to this lawsuit, and that I served the within Summons in said County on the _____ day of _____, _____, by delivering a copy thereof, with copy of Petition attached, in the following manner: (check one box and fill in appropriate blanks)

❑ to Respondent.

❑ to _____, a person over ____ years of age and residing at the residence of Respondent, _____, who was not home at the time of service.

❑ by posting a copy of the Summons and Petition in a public part of the premises of Respondent _____ (used if no person found at dwelling house or usual place of abode, if permitted by state law)

_____   _____
Signature of Person Making Service   Title [if any]

SUBSCRIBED AND SWORN to before me this _____ day of _____, _____.

_____
Notary or Other Officer authorized to Administer Oaths

Index

A

abandonment, 16, 145
abuse, 16, 17, 24, 30, 31, 45, 75,
    89, 90, 91, 92, 93, 94, 95, 150
acknowledgment of parentage,
    16, 53
admission of documents, 85
adoption, 2, 16, 98, 150
affidavit of paternity, 16
affidavit of service, 58
after-school activities, 22, 99
agreement to cooperate, 36, 42
Aid to Families with Dependent
    Children (AFDC), 99
alcohol, 25, 30, 31
alimony, 56, 68, 105, 110, 120,
    121
alleged father, 16
alternative dispute resolution
    (ADR), 41, 67

American Bar Association, 11,
    68, 70
annulment, 50, 52, 131
appeals, 27, 33, 141, 143, 145,
    147, 149, 150, 151
arbitration, 67, 68
arrest record, 30, 45
assets, 22, 79, 101, 110
attorneys, 3, 6, 7, 8, 9, 10, 11, 47,
    52, 70, 71, 73, 77, 78, 80, 81,
    82, 86, 93, 99, 134
    fees, 10, 11
    finding, 7
    firing, 11

B

baby-sitters, 27, 65, 90
bar associations, 8

best interests of the child, 2, 14, 18, 19, 20, 21, 22, 23, 25, 26, 27, 29, 30, 31, 32, 33, 34, 35, 36, 40, 51, 67, 68, 72, 74, 103, 112, 117, 118, 123, 139, 142, 143, 144, 145, 151

birthdays, 81, 84, 85

brainstorming, 65, 151

C

caption, 55, 60

case reporter, 4

case style, 55

central registries, 98

Child Support Calculation Worksheets, 135

circuit court, 54, 55

civil cases, 6, 67, 80

clear and convincing standard, 137

closing argument, 87

clothing, 22, 44, 99, 133

codes, 3, 5, 20, 70

combined income, 107, 108, 110, 119, 121, 128

Combined Income Child Support Worksheet, 119, 128

complaint, 10, 16, 52, 53, 54, 55, 131

conciliation, 67

conferences, 22, 44, 81, 84

confidentiality, 7, 74

cooperation, 25, 36, 43, 71

counseling, 17, 68

counterclaim, 139

court orders, 1, 16, 27, 37, 52, 60, 91, 92, 93, 95, 102, 112, 113, 125, 132, 145, 149
    preventive, 91

crime, 24, 90

cross-examination, 82, 87

custodians, 1, 14, 17, 18, 20, 97, 134

Custody and Visitation Checklist, 66

D

day care, 65, 90, 133

de facto parent, 14, 17, 18, 32, 33

death of a parent, 149

debts, 104, 111

default, 60, 140

dependency exemption, 18, 111, 116

deposition, 80

digest, 6

disability, 105, 111, 120

discipline, 15, 23, 29, 44

discovery, 79, 80

dissolution of marriage, 50

divorce, 1, 2, 5, 7, 8, 13, 23, 34, 35, 47, 50, 52, 55, 56, 67, 68, 73, 93, 99, 101, 102, 113, 131

DNA, 16, 137

doctor, 22, 27, 38, 49, 81

due diligence, 59

duration of the order, 124

E

earning capacity, 23, 106, 132

economic resources, 22

education, 15, 22, 38, 66, 73, 74, 99, 102, 105, 106, 124, 133, 139

electronic funds transfer (EFT), 125

employment, 48, 101, 120, 132, 136, 143, 144, 147, 148

environment, 15, 17, 20, 23, 24, 26, 27, 45, 141, 142, 143, 145 establishing parentage, 131, 136

evidence, 29, 51, 85, 86, 87, 137, 140, 146

exchange of the child, 72, 94

exhibits, 85, 86, 87

extended family, 1, 23, 45, 97

extraordinary expenses, 102, 103, 106, 109, 110, 143, 147

F

family law, 5, 6, 7, 8, 10, 11, 61, 67, 69, 79, 150

family support order, 99

Federal Parent Locator Service, 92, 136

filing fees, 51, 53, 134

Final Judgment, 87, 88

Financial Affidavit, 132, 139

financial resources, 7, 101, 104, 118

fit and proper parent, 19, 20, 78

Fletcher v. Fletcher, 28

flexibility, 2, 23, 39, 67, 68

friends, 7, 23, 26, 42, 83, 90, 135

G

grandparents, 1, 14, 23, 33, 34, 37, 50, 67, 97, 145

gross income, 105, 106, 107, 108, 110, 111, 119, 120, 128, 129, 147

guardian ad litem, 69, 78

guidelines, 1, 2, 42, 78, 98, 100, 101, 103, 104, 105, 106, 107, 108, 109, 110, 111, 112, 113, 114, 115, 118, 119, 120, 121, 122, 123, 124, 126, 128, 129, 133, 139, 140, 147, 148, 150, 151

H

health, 15, 20, 25, 38, 45, 49, 65, 73, 77, 101, 102, 106, 118, 121, 123, 126, 128, 129, 133, 138, 145

health insurance, 101, 102, 106, 121, 128, 129

hearsay, 83

holidays, 37, 43, 72, 93, 143

housing, 99, 122, 133

I

illness, 22, 38, 44, 49, 81

In re Parentage of J.S., 100

income shares model, 107

income withholding, 125

injury, 38

Internal Revenue Service (IRS), 18, 111, 116, 136

interrogatories, 66, 79, 80

J

joint custody, 15, 18, 27, 33, 41, 42, 43, 113

judges, 7, 20, 26, 35, 36, 40, 41, 61, 77, 78, 81, 82, 85, 86, 87, 88, 117, 122, 131, 138, 145, 150

judgment, 10, 36, 40, 54, 87, 88, 117, 131, 146, 150

jurisdiction, 2, 32, 51, 52, 54, 56, 57, 58, 60, 91, 93, 141, 142

K

kidnapping, 24, 31, 89, 90, 91, 92, 93, 95

L

law library, 3, 5, 57
legal custody, 15, 37, 65, 99
    joint, 15, 65
legal research, 3, 34, 103
legal separation, 50, 52, 131
life insurance, 118, 126, 127, 133, 136, 138, 149
lifestyle issues, 21, 28
location, 27, 32, 37, 43, 51, 55, 58, 59, 79, 94, 125, 134
love and affection, 21, 44

M

maintenance, 56, 68, 105, 110, 120, 121, 133, 138
mediation, 41, 43, 60, 61, 62, 63, 64, 65, 66, 67, 68, 69, 70, 71, 72, 73, 74, 75, 77, 95
Medicaid, 99
medical care, 15, 22
Meldrum v. Novotny, 33
military, 118, 124, 149
misconduct, 30, 31, 101, 144
modification, 141
moral fitness, 24, 28
Motion for Temporary Relief, 60-61, 138
moving, 27, 40, 43, 143, 144
Mullins v. Mullins, 29

N

name change, 29, 30
needs of the child, 97, 101, 118, 138
neglect, 16, 94
net income, 105, 106, 107, 109, 119, 120, 121
noncustodial parent, 15, 18, 40, 93, 99, 102, 106, 107, 108, 109, 110, 112, 143, 144
nonparents, 14, 17, 19, 32, 33, 52
nontraditional families, 13, 68
notice of action, 59

O

order, 1, 3, 4, 6, 7, 26, 27, 33, 35, 40, 42, 43, 53, 54, 55, 60, 61, 72, 78, 80, 82, 85, 87, 88, 89, 90, 91, 92, 93, 94, 95, 97, 99, 101, 102, 111, 112, 113, 115, 118, 123, 124, 125, 127, 128, 129, 131, 132, 135, 136, 137, 138, 139, 141, 142, 144, 145, 146, 147, 148, 149, 150
Order for Temporary Relief, 61, 138
Order Modifying Judgment, 88
out-of-state parent, 91, 135, 136

P

Palmore v. Sidoti, 29
parent/child relationship, 2, 7, 19, 21, 23, 25, 28, 29, 30, 31, 32, 33, 34, 40, 56, 64, 67, 68, 74, 80, 81, 82, 92, 144
parental care, 21, 44
parental information, 48

Parental Kidnapping Prevention Act (PKPA), 92

parenting agreements, 15, 38, 42, 43
    joint, 42, 43

Parenting Plan, 35, 36, 37, 39, 41, 43, 45, 70, 72, 93, 94

parenting time, 43, 53, 113

past-due support, 148, 150

paternity, 16, 53, 54, 56, 57, 60, 98, 99, 134, 136, 137

payments, 70, 99, 105, 115, 118, 120, 121, 125, 126, 133, 134, 148

percentage income guidelines, 107, 109, 115, 119, 121, 129

Percentage of Income Child Support Worksheet, 119, 129

permanence, 23, 45

Personal Responsibility and Work Opportunity Reconciliation Act, 98

petition, 10, 34, 51, 52, 53, 54, 55, 56, 57, 58, 59, 60, 61, 88, 93, 132, 134, 135, 138, 139, 140, 146, 148

Petition for Custody, 52, 53, 54, 55, 56, 57, 58, 59, 60, 61, 132

Petition to Modify Judgment of Custody and/or Child Support, 88, 146

physical custody, 15, 18, 37, 65
    joint, 15

posttrial proceedings, 150

preexisting child support order, 112

preparation for your case, 48

preponderance of the evidence, 51, 137

primary caregiver, 17

prorate, 108, 109, 115, 126

protective orders, 89, 93

psychological parent, 14, 17

putative father, 16

Q

qualified domestic relations order, 139

qualified medical child support order, 138

R

reasonable care, 1

reasonable visitation, 32, 37, 94

religion, 15, 21, 22, 27, 28, 66, 143

remarriage, 43, 143, 148, 150

report card, 85, 86

request for admissions, 79

residential parent, 111, 112

Response, 11, 60

responsibility, 2, 11, 14, 15, 22, 37, 44, 94, 98, 99, 103, 104, 112

retirement, 105, 106, 120, 121, 125, 128, 129, 132, 139

return of service, 58, 59

S

safety, 24

salary, 120, 125, 132

same-sex parents, 1, 13, 14, 18, 68, 97

schedules, 15, 34, 39, 48, 53, 64, 70, 72, 108, 114, 121, 126, 141

school, 3, 15, 20, 22, 25, 26, 30, 36, 37, 38, 42, 44, 48, 49, 64, 65, 72, 78, 81, 83, 84, 85, 86, 90, 99, 102, 124, 133, 145, 149

security, 24, 45, 48, 49, 91, 105, 106, 118, 120, 126, 128, 129, 135, 136, 137, 138, 139

service by publication, 59

severe emotional distress, 75

shared parenting, 15, 113, 114

Social Security, 48, 49, 91, 105, 106, 120, 128, 129, 135, 136, 137

sole custody, 15, 18, 26, 43, 63, 64, 65, 83, 93, 115

special needs, 44, 111

split custody, 15, 26, 65, 115

spring vacations, 37

stability, 23, 45, 68, 142, 146

standard of living, 100, 101, 104, 118

State Parent Locator Service (SPLS), 135

statutes, 3, 4, 5, 20, 33, 119, 139, 149
    annotated, 3, 4

statutory custody factors, 20

stepparents, 14, 32, 33, 97, 143

Subpoena, 80, 83

substantial change in circumstances, 10, 111, 142, 143, 146, 147

summer vacations, 36, 37

Summons, 10, 52, 54, 57, 58, 59, 60, 61

supervised visitation, 94

T

taxes, 18, 106, 116, 119, 120, 128, 129, 133
    exemption, 115, 118, 127

tender-years doctrine, 14

termination, 16, 141, 143, 145, 147, 148, 149, 151

testimony, 80, 81, 83, 85, 87, 138, 150

transportation, 37, 40, 44, 45, 72, 115, 122, 133, 144

travel, 39, 48, 63, 72, 144

trial, 26, 33, 45, 61, 63, 65, 67, 69, 71, 73, 75, 79, 80, 92, 146, 150

Troxel v. Granville, 33

tryout period, 50, 66, 67

U

unfit parents, 16

Uniform Child Custody Jurisdiction Act (UCCJA), 51, 52, 57, 91, 142

Uniform Child Custody Jurisdiction Enforcement Act (UCCJEA), 52, 91, 142

Uniform Interstate Family Support Act (UIFSA), 98, 136

unwed parents, 16

utilities, 133

V

vacations, 37, 43, 50, 72, 93

venue, 51

violence, 20, 24, 31, 72, 75, 89, 92, 93

visitation centers, 94

visitation schedule, 39, 48
    violations, 40, 41

W

wealth, 21

winter vacations, 37

witnesses, 79, 83, 85, 87, 94, 146
    expert, 83, 85

work patterns, 21